U.S. Department of Justice
Office of Justice Programs

Bureau of Justice Statistics
Special Report

I0448778

August 2007, NCJ 218914

Prison Rape Elimination Act of 2003

Sexual Violence Reported by Correctional Authorities, 2006

By Allen J. Beck, Ph.D.
Paige M. Harrison, BJS Statisticians
and Devon B. Adams, Policy Analyst

The Prison Rape Elimination Act of 2003 (P.L. 108-79) requires the Bureau of Justice Statistics (BJS) to develop new national data collections on the incidence and prevalence of sexual violence within correctional facilities. This report fulfills the requirement under Sec. 4 (c)(1) of the Act for submission of an annual report on the activities of BJS with respect to prison rape.

Between January 1 and June 30, 2007, BJS completed the third annual national survey of administrative records in adult correctional facilities, covering calendar year 2006. Although the results were limited to incidents reported to correctional officials, the survey provides an understanding of what officials know, based on the number of reported allegations, and the outcomes of follow-up investigations.[1] By comparing results of the 2006 survey with those from 2004 and 2005, BJS is able to assess trends in sexual violence for the first time since the Act was passed.

Administrative records surveys are one part of BJS's multi-measure, multi-mode implementation strategy. During 2006, BJS completed development and testing of survey methodologies that rely on reports of victimization provided directly by prison and jail inmates, former inmates, and youth held in juvenile facilities. These methodologies rely on self-administered surveys that offer anonymity to victims of sexual violence to report their experiences. Using Audio Computer-Assisted Self-Interview procedures, respondents interact with a computer-administered questionnaire using a touch-screen and follow audio instructions delivered via headphones. (See box on page 2 for a status report and national implementation schedule.)

The 2006 administrative records survey provides the basis for the annual statistical review required under the Act. The survey included all Federal and State prison systems and facilities operated by the U.S. military and Immigration and Customs Enforcement. The survey also included representative samples of jail jurisdictions, privately operated adult prisons and jails, and jails in Indian country. Altogether, the administrative survey included facilities housing more than 1.8 million inmates, or 81% of all inmates held in adult facilities in 2006. (See *Methodology* for detailed sampling description.)

As with previous administrative records surveys, the 2006 survey results should not be used to rank systems or facilities. Given the absence of uniform reporting, caution is necessary for accurate interpretation of the survey results. Higher or lower counts among facilities may reflect variations in definitions, reporting capacities, and procedures for recording allegations as opposed to differences in the underlying incidence of sexual violence.

In 2004 BJS developed uniform definitions of sexual violence. Incidents of inmate-on-inmate sexual violence were classified as either *nonconsensual sexual acts* (the most serious violent forms of sexual assault) or *abusive sexual contacts* (less serious, but unwanted). Incidents involving staff were separated into *staff sexual misconduct* (any act of a sexual nature directed toward an inmate) or *staff sexual harassment* (repeated verbal statements of a sexual nature to an inmate). For this report, all such incidents are considered sexual violence. (See *Methodology* for detailed definitions.)

Detailed tabulations of the survey results by system and sampled facility are presented in Appendix tables 1a – 4b, available on the BJS web site at <http://www.ojp.usdoj.gov/bjs/pub/pdf/svrca06.pdf>.

---

[1]A survey of State-operated juvenile systems and privately or locally operated juvenile facilities was also conducted for 2006. Results from the 2005 and 2006 juvenile surveys will be published in a separate report.

Allegations of sexual violence rose during 2006

Reports of sexual violence varied across systems and sampled facilities, with every State prison system except Alaska and New Mexico reporting at least one allegation of sexual violence. Among the 344 sampled local jail jurisdictions participating in the survey, 161 (47%) reported an allegation. About 52% of the 46 sampled privately operated prisons and jails reported at least one allegation.

The 2006 survey recorded 5,605 allegations of sexual violence. Taking into account weights for sampled facilities, the estimated total number of allegations for the Nation was 6,528. Since the Prison Rape Elimination Act was passed in 2003, the estimated number of allegations nationwide has risen by 21% (5,386 in 2004; 6,241 in 2005). Some of the increase may have resulted from adoption of BJS definitions and improved reporting by correctional authorities.

Collection of victim self-report of sexual violence in prisons and jails underway

BJS is working toward full implementation of the Prison Rape Elimination Act. As of June 30, 2007, BJS and its data collection agents had completed all phases of development and testing. BJS has entered into cooperative agreements to collect reports of sexual violence directly from inmates in prisons and jails, former State prison inmates, and youth in State juvenile facilities. BJS has worked extensively with -

1. Research Triangle International (RTI) (Raleigh, NC) to collect data from inmates in prisons and jails;

2. Westat, Inc. (Rockville, MD) to collect data from adjuducated youth in State and local juvenile facilities;

3. National Opinion Research Center (NORC) (Chicago, IL) to collect data from State inmates under active parole supervision.

Though underlying survey methodology and logistical procedures differ with each of these data collections, the measurement strategies are consistent. The surveys consist of an Audio Computer-Assisted Self-Interview (ACASI) in which respondents interact with a computer-administered questionnaire using a touch-screen and follow audio instructions delivered via headphones. The use of ACASI is expected to overcome many limitations of previous research.

The following work has been completed or is underway:

Prison and jail inmates

• Implementation of the National Inmate Survey (NIS) began in April 2007 in 148 prisons and 302 jails. Data collection will continue through December 2007, with about 90,000 completed interviews anticipated.

• On August 30, 2007, BJS will consult with corrections administrators and experts in statistical scaling to discuss various measures of sexual violence by which to rank facilities.

• Rankings of prison facilities, as required under the Act, are expected in November 2007; jail rankings are expected shortly after the completion of the data collection.

Youth in custody

• Testing of the National Survey of Youth in Custody (NSYC) was completed in June 2007. The test involved 12 juvenile facilities in 6 States with more than 750 completed interviews.

• Results of the testing and plans for implementation will be presented to juvenile administrators, researchers, and other stakeholders at a national workshop on August 28, 2007.

• National implementation is expected in early 2008, pending approval from the Office of Management and Budget (OMB). When fully implemented, the NSYC will include about 15,000 adjudicated youth in a sample of 208 State-operated facilities and 48 large non-State facilities (that had an average daily population of 90 or more youth during 2005).

Former State prisoners

• The Former Prisoner Survey (FPS) was tested in 16 parole offices with 788 former inmates on active parole supervision. In May 2007, the collection was submitted to OMB for review.

• The survey will provide a national estimate of the incidence and prevalence of sexual victimization based on reports of former State prison inmates. Data will be collected on the totality of the prior term of incarceration, including any time in a police lockup, local jail, State prison, or community correctional facility prior to final discharge.

• National implementation will begin in late 2007, pending OMB approval. When fully implemented the survey will include about 16,500 former inmates in a sample of 285 parole offices.

Expressed as rates, there were 2.91 allegations of sexual violence per 1,000 inmates held in prison, jail, and other adult correctional facilities in 2006, up from 2.46 per 1,000 inmates in 2004. Overall, the rate in State prisons (3.75 per 1,000) was higher than the rate in local jails (2.05 per 1,000) (table 1).

About 36% of the reported allegations of sexual violence in 2006 involved staff sexual misconduct; 34%, inmate-on-inmate nonconsensual sexual acts; 17%, staff sexual harassment; and 13%, inmate-on-inmate abusive sexual contacts. These percentages were nearly unchanged from those reported in 2005. Correctional authorities reported

3,489 allegations of staff sexual misconduct and harass-ment during 2006, compared to 3,470 during 2005.[2]

Allegations of sexual violence, by type of incident, 2005 and 2006

Incident type	National estimate		Percent	
	2006	2005	2006	2005
Total	6,528	6,241	100%	100%
Inmate-on-inmate noncon-sensual sexual acts	2,205	2,160	34	35
Inmate-on-inmate abusive sexual contacts	834	611	13	10
Staff sexual misconduct	2,371	2,386	36	38
Staff sexual harassment	1,118	1,084	17	17

Table 1. Allegations of sexual violence and rates per 1,000 inmates, by type of facility, 2005 and 2006

Facility type	National estimate		Rate per 1,000 inmates	
	2006	2005	2006	2005
Total	6,528	6,241	2.91	2.83
Prisons				
Public-Federal[a]	242	268	1.50	1.71
Public-State	4,516	4,341	3.75	3.68
Private	200	182	1.91	1.80
Local jails				
Public	1,521	1,384	2.05	1.86
Private	12	22	0.72	1.33
Other adult facilities				
Indian country jails[b]	29	32	^	^
Military-operated	3	8	^	^
ICE-operated	5	4	^	^

^Too few cases to provide a reliable rate.

[a]Federal numbers for 2006 are not comparable to those in 2005 due to a change in reporting.

[b]Excludes facilities housing juveniles only.

Upon investigation, most allegations were unsubstantiated or unfounded

The most common outcome of investigations was a deter-mination that the evidence was insufficient to show whether the alleged incident occurred. In 2006 more than half of all allegations (55%) were unsubstantiated; more than a quar-ter (29%) were unfounded (determined not to have occurred). About a sixth of all allegations (17%) were sub-stantiated. Previous surveys recorded similar outcomes.

Based on completed investigations, allegations of staff sex-ual harassment and inmate-on-inmate nonconsensual sex-ual acts were less likely to have been substantiated than other types of allegations (table 2). During 2006, 7% of alle-gations of staff sexual harassment and 14% of inmate-on-inmate nonconsensual sexual acts were substantiated, compared to 19% of the allegations of inmate-on-inmate abusive sexual contacts and 25% of the allegations of staff sexual misconduct.

[2]See Sexual Violence Reported by Correctional Authorities, 2005 at <http://www.ojp.usdoj.gov/bjs/abstract/svrca05.htm>.

Table 2. Outcomes of investigations into allegations of sexual violence, by type of facility, 2006

	All facilities[a]		State and Federal prisons		Local jails		Private prisons and jails	
	Number	Percent[b]	Number	Percent[b]	Number	Percent[b]	Number	Percent[b]
Inmate-on-inmate nonconsensual sexual acts	2,205	100%	1,390	100%	725	100%	87	100%
Substantiated	262	14	147	13	111	17	3	4
Unsubstantiated	1,030	54	707	61	295	44	28	34
Unfounded	616	32	304	26	259	39	52	63
Investigation ongoing	297		232		60		4	
Inmate-on-inmate abusive sexual contacts	834	100%	707	100%	116	100%	11	100%
Substantiated	158	19	125	18	31	27	0	0
Unsubstantiated	491	60	426	62	54	48	9	100
Unfounded	165	21	139	20	28	25	0	0
Investigation ongoing	20		17		2		1	
Staff sexual misconduct	2,371	100%	1,677	100%	575	100%	95	100%
Substantiated	471	25	235	18	229	47	15	17
Unsubstantiated	877	47	745	58	91	19	36	41
Unfounded	535	28	309	24	166	34	37	42
Investigation ongoing	489		388		90		9	
Staff sexual harassment	1,118	100%	984	100%	105	100%	19	100%
Substantiated	70	7	47	6	15	15	0	0
Unsubstantiated	595	62	537	64	50	51	7	100
Unfounded	292	31	258	31	34	34	0	0
Investigation ongoing	161		142		6		12	

Note: Detail may not sum to total due to rounding.

[a]Includes jails in Indian country and facilities operated by the U.S. military and Immigration and Customs Enforcement (ICE).

[b]Percents based on allegations for which investigations have been completed.

Overall, 967 incidents of sexual violence were substantiated in 2006, compared to 885 in 2005 (table 3). Relative to the number of inmates, the rate of substantiated incidents of sexual violence in 2006 was 4.3 per 10,000 inmates, nearly unchanged from the 4.0 per 10,000 inmates recorded in 2005. Rates were lowest in Federal prisons and privately operated prisons (fewer than 1 in 10,000). Rates of substantiated incidents in State prisons, local jail jurisdictions, and privately operated jails were 4 to 5 times higher. Substantiated incidents were too few to provide reliable estimates for other types of facilities.

Surveys reveal consistent patterns of sexual violence in correctional facilities

In 2005 and 2006, correctional authorities were asked to provide detailed information on all substantiated incidents of sexual violence on a separate incident form. Authorities reported information on the circumstances of each incident, characteristics of victims and perpetrators, type of pressure or physical force, sanctions imposed, and victim assistance. The two surveys provide a profile of victims and perpetrators and reveal consistent patterns among the substantiated incidents.

Data provided on incidents of inmate-on-inmate sexual violence revealed that —

• More than one inmate was reported to have been victimized in 8% of the incidents in 2006 and 4% of those in 2005 (table 4).
• More than one perpetrator was involved in 10% of the incidents in 2006 and 7% of those in 2005.
• Males constituted 82% of the victims and 85% of the perpetrators in 2006, compared to 88% of the victims and 91% of the perpetrators in 2005.
• In both years, victims were on average younger than perpetrators. In 2006, 44% of victims were age 24 or younger, while 81% of perpetrators were age 25 or older.

• In 2006 whites made up 72% of the victims; blacks, 16%; and Hispanics, 9%. Among perpetrators, 39% were white; 49% black; and 10% Hispanics. Similar distributions were observed in 2005.
• In both years at least half of inmate-on-inmate sexual violence was interracial: 6% of incidents in 2006 involved a white perpetrator and a non-white victim; 35%, a black perpetrator and a non-black victim; and 8%, a Hispanic perpetrator and a non-Hispanic victim (not shown in table).

Number of victims and perpetrators by race/
Hispanic origin

| | Perpetrator | | | |
Victim	White*	Black*	Hispanic	Other*
Total	200	227	52	8
White*	171	146	32	7
Black*	9	58	7	0
Hispanic	14	19	11	0
Other*	6	4	2	1

*Excludes persons of Hispanic origin.

Table 4. Characteristics of victims and perpetrators in substantiated incidents of inmate-on-inmate sexual violence, 2005 and 2006

	2006	2005
Victim characteristics		
Number of victims		
1	92%	96%
2 or more	8	4
Gender		
Male	82%	88%
Female	18	12
Age		
Under 25	44%	53%
25-39	40	39
40 or older	15	8
Race/Hispanic origin		
White[a]	72%	73%
Black[a]	16	12
Hispanic	9	9
Other[a,b]	3	6
Perpetrator characteristics		
Number of perpetrators		
1	90%	93%
2 or more	10	7
Gender		
Male	85%	91%
Female	15	9
Age		
Under 25	20%	26%
25-39	53	44
40 or older	28	30
Race/Hispanic origin		
White[a]	39%	43%
Black[a]	49	39
Hispanic	10	15
Other[a,b]	2	3

[a]Excludes victims and perpetrators of Hispanic origin.
[b]Includes American Indians, Alaska Natives, Asians, Native Hawaiians, and Other Pacific Islanders.

Table 3. Substantiated incidents of sexual violence and rates per 1,000 inmates, by type of facility, 2005 and 2006

| | National estimate | | Rate per 1,000 inmates | |
Facility type	2006	2005	2006	2005
Total	967	885	0.43	0.40
Prisons				
Public-Federal	5	41	0.03	0.26
Public-State	549	458	0.46	0.39
Private	9	24	0.09	0.24
Local jails				
Public	385	336	0.52	0.45
Private	8	13	0.48	0.78
Other adult facilities				
Indian country jails*	7	10	^	^
Military-operated	2	2	^	^
ICE-operated	2	1	^	^

^Too few cases to provide a reliable rate.
*Excludes facilities housing juveniles only.

Most incidents of sexual violence among inmates involve force or threat of force and occur in the victim's cell, in the evening

Correctional authorities reported that physical force or threat of force was used in more than half of all substantiated incidents of inmate-on-inmate sexual violence (table 5). In 21% of the incidents in 2006, no force was used or threatened. In 30% of incidents, victims were talked into it. In 7% of incidents, victims were offered protection, bribed, or blackmailed.

Force or the threat of force was more common among incidents of nonconsensual sexual acts (67%) than among incidents of abusive sexual contact (44%). The victim was held down or restrained in 38% of the incidents of nonconsensual sexual acts during 2006. In 18% of these incidents, the victim was physically harmed or injured. Although abusive sexual contacts are typically less serious forms of assault, the victim was held down or restrained in 28% of the incidents, and the victim was physically harmed or injured in 10% of the incidents (not shown in table).

Overall, the use or threat of force was more prevalent among incidents reported in 2006 (58%) than in 2005 (51%). In addition, the proportion of victims who were injured rose, from 15% in 2005 to 20% in 2006. Anal or rectal tearing was reported at nearly the same levels (5% in 2006 and 6% in 2005).

Incidents of sexual violence among inmates occurred most often in a victim's cell or dormitory (totaling more than 70% in both years). By contrast, 17% of the incidents in 2006 and 21% of the incidents in 2005 occurred in a common area, such as a shower or dayroom. In 6% of the incidents in 2006 and 9% in 2005, the location was a program service area, such as a storage room, hallway, laundry, cafeteria, kitchen, or workshop.

Sexual violence among inmates was more common in the evening (between 6 p.m. and midnight) than at any other time of the day, exceeding 40% of all incidents in both surveys. In 2005 it was least common between midnight and 6 a.m. (18%); in 2006 it was least common between 6 a.m. and noon (20%).

Incidents of sexual violence among inmates, when reported, are typically reported by a victim or another inmate and not by a correctional officer or other staff. In 2006, 83% of the substantiated incidents of inmate sexual violence were reported by the victim or another inmate; in 2005, 91%.

Table 5. Circumstances surrounding substantiated incidents of inmate-on-inmate sexual violence, by type, 2005 and 2006

	All types		Nonconsensual sexual acts		Abusive sexual contacts	
Number of incidents	2006	2005	2006	2005	2006	2005
Type of pressure or force						
None	21%	30%	14%	18%	31%	57%
Force/threat of force	58	51	67	59	44	33
Persuasion or talked into it	30	18	32	22	28	10
Other	7	17	8	22	4	8
Victim injured						
No	80%	85%	74%	78%	87%	97%
Yes	20	15	26	22	13	3
Where occurred						
In victim's cell/room	64%	59%	76%	59%	46%	59%
In a dormitory	9	12	6	11	14	15
In a common area	17	21	11	23	26	16
Other areas	13	14	10	10	17	24
Time of day[b]						
6 a.m. to noon	20%	28%	17%	22%	24%	41%
Noon to 6 p.m.	26	20	18	18	37	25
6 p.m. to midnight	45	44	47	50	41	31
Midnight to 6 a.m.	26	18	32	18	17	18
Who reported the incident						
Victim	70%	83%	72%	84%	65%	79%
Another inmate	13	8	16	8	9	10
Correctional officer	17	11	12	11	24	10
Other	4	6	2	6	7	4

Note: Detail may sum to more than 100% because multiple responses were allowed for each item.

Most victims experienced a change in their housing; most inmate perpetrators received solitary confinement

The most common response to a reported incident of sexual violence among inmates was to place the victim in administrative segregation or protective custody and to move the perpetrator to solitary confinement or other higher level of custody. Among victims of inmate sexual violence reported in the 2006 survey, 40% were placed in administrative segregation or protective custody; 13% were placed in a medical unit; and 16% were transferred to another facility (not shown in table). Nearly a quarter (24%) experienced no change in their housing or custody level. Among victims in the 2005 survey, nearly the same actions had been taken; a slightly higher percent (32%) had experienced no change in housing.

Inmate perpetrators were moved to solitary confinement in 78% of the incidents of sexual violence in 2006, compared to 71% in 2005 (table 6). Perpetrators of the most serious incidents, nonconsensual sexual acts, were the most likely to receive solitary confinement (81% in 2006, 72% in 2005).

Legal sanctions, including arrest, referral for prosecution, or a new sentence, were imposed on perpetrators in 41% of the incidents in 2006 and 51% of the incidents in 2005. This drop was attributed to a decline in legal sanctions imposed on perpetrators of abusive sexual contacts (39% in 2005; 18% in 2006).

In addition, perpetrators in 2006 received a combination of other sanctions, including confinement to their cell or room (16%), loss of privileges (20%), placement in a higher custody level (22%), and transfer to another facility (22%). These types of sanctions were imposed in 2005 at similar rates, except for confinement to their cell or room (28%).

The sexual relationship "appeared to be willing" in 57% of incidents of staff sexual misconduct and harassment

Correctional authorities also reported detailed data on 544 substantiated incidents of staff sexual misconduct and harassment (up from 344 in 2005). To address concerns about the reporting and interpretation of data in the 2005 survey, BJS changed the item related to the nature of the incidents in 2006. The option "*Romantic*" was replaced by "*Sexual relationship between inmate and staff appeared to be willing.*" The options "*Other*" and "*Level of coercion unknown*" were added. In addition, the options were re-ordered from most to least coercive. (See *Methodology* for further details.)

Though these changes were introduced in 2006, the findings remained similar to those reported in 2005.

• The sexual relationship "appeared to be willing" in 57% of incidents in 2006 (table 7). In comparison, the relationship was classified as "romantic" in 68% of the incidents in 2005.
• Physical force, abuse of power, or pressure was involved in 7% of the incidents in 2006, compared to 15% of the incidents in 2005.
• A third of the incidents in 2006 involved other forms of assault, including sexual harassment (15%), indecent exposure/invasion of privacy (9%), and unwanted touching for sexual gratification (5%).
• In 12% of the incidents in 2006, correctional authorities reported the "level of coercion unknown."

Table 6. Sanctions imposed on perpetrators in substantiated incidents of inmate-on-inmate sexual violence, by type of incident, 2005 and 2006

	All incidents		Nonconsensual sexual acts		Abusive sexual contacts	
	2006	2005	2006	2005	2006	2005
Solitary/disciplinary	78%	71%	81%	72%	75%	70%
Legal action	41	51	56	58	18	39
Arrested	16	12	21	16	6	4
Referred for prosecution	33	46	46	51	13	35
Confined to own cell/room	16	28	18	25	12	33
Placed in higher custody	22	20	24	27	20	5
Loss of privileges	20	21	23	22	16	19
Transferred to another facility	22	19	24	18	17	21

Note: Detail may sum to more than 100% because multiple sanctions may have been imposed.

Table 7. Characteristics of substantiated incidents of staff sexual misconduct and harassment, by type of facility, 2006

Characteristic	All facilities[a]	Prison	Jail
Number of incidents	544	282	239
Nature of the incident[b]			
Relationship appeared to be willing	57%	62%	51%
Sexual harassment	15	16	15
Unwanted touching	5	9	2
Indecent exposure	9	2	18
Pressure/abuse of power	5	7	2
Physical force	2	2	0
Other/unknown	12	9	16
Number of staff involved[c]			
1	98%	98%	98%
2	2	2	2
Number of victims[c]			
1	83%	89%	74%
2	14	5	25
3	2	2	0
4 or more	2	3	0

[a]Includes substantiated incidents reported by private prisons and jails, Indian country jails, and facilities operated by the U.S. military and ICE.

[b]Detail may sum to more than 100% because multiple responses were allowed for each item.

[c]Detail may not sum to 100% due to rounding.

Other data reported on substantiated incidents of staff sexual misconduct and harassment during 2006 revealed that —

- In more than half of the incidents, the victim (29%) or another inmate (27%) reported the misconduct (table 8).
- Most incidents occurred outside the inmate's living area: 46% in a program area, 8% in a common area, and 8% outside of the facility.
- Incidents occurred most often between noon and 6 p.m. in prisons (53%) and between 6 p.m. and midnight in local jails (74%).
- More than one staff member was involved in the sexual misconduct in 2% of the incidents.
- Staff had victimized more than one inmate in 18% of the incidents.

Female staff more frequently implicated in sexual misconduct in prisons; male staff in local jails

In the 2006 survey, characteristics of victims and perpetrators of staff sexual misconduct and harassment differed by type of facility:

- In State and Federal prisons, 65% of inmate victims of staff sexual misconduct and harassment were male, while 58% of staff perpetrators were female (tables 9 and 10).
- In local jails, 80% of victims were female, while 79% of perpetrators were male.
- 49% of staff perpetrators in prisons were age 40 or older, while 65% of victims were under age 35.
- 56% of staff perpetrators in jails were age 40 or older, while 86% of victims were under age 35.
- Among staff perpetrators in prisons and jails, 71% were white; 20%, black; and 7%, Hispanic. Among inmate victims, 66% were white; 23%, black; and 8%, Hispanic.
- A correctional officer was identified as the perpetrator in 54% of incidents in prisons, and in 98% of incidents in jails (table 11).
- A contract employee was involved in 17% of the incidents in prisons and in 2% of those in jails.

Table 8. Circumstances of substantiated incidents of staff sexual misconduct and harassment, by type of facility, 2006

Circumstance	All facilities[a]	Prison	Jail
Who reported the incident[b]			
Victim	29%	29%	29%
Another inmate	27	23	29
Family of victim	8	2	16
Correctional officer	25	27	21
Administrative staff	8	11	4
Medical/healthcare staff	1	2	0
Instructor/teacher/counselor	1	1	1
Other (anonymous/letter)	3	5	1
Where occurred			
In victim's cell/room	10%	9%	13%
In a dormitory	14	10	20
In a common area	8	10	4
In temporary holding area	8	0	18
In a program service area	46	49	41
Outside the facility	8	12	3
In transit	<1	<1	<1
Staff office/infirmary	5	9	1
Other/unknown	7	9	6
Time of day			
6 a.m. to noon	35%	38%	36%
Noon to 6 p.m.	32	53	11
6 p.m. to midnight	56	38	74
Midnight to 6 a.m.	14	16	12

Note: Detail may sum to more than 100% because multiple responses were allowed for each item.

[a]Includes substantiated incidents reported by private prisons and jails, Indian country jails, and facilities operated by the U.S. military and ICE.

[b]The category "Chaplain/other religious official" was not marked in any incident.

Table 9. Characteristics of inmates involved in staff sexual misconduct and harassment, by type of facility, 2006

Characteristic	All facilities[a]	Prison	Jail
Gender[b]			
Male	44%	65%	20%
Female	56	35	80
Age[b]			
Under 18	0%	0%	0%
18-24	18	16	21
25-29	33	29	38
30-34	25	20	27
35-39	13	21	6
40-44	8	9	7
45 or older	3	5	1
Race/Hispanic origin			
White[c]	66%	54%	80%
Black[c]	23	32	14
Hispanic	8	12	5
Other[c,d]	3	2	1

[a]Includes substantiated incidents reported by private prisons and jails, Indian country jails, and facilities operated by the U.S. military and ICE.

[b]The number of victims of staff misconduct totaled 671: gender was reported for 636; age for 631; and race/Hispanic origin for 628.

[c]Excludes inmates of Hispanic origin.

[d]Includes American Indians, Alaska Natives, Asians, Native Hawaiians, and Other Pacific Islanders.

Table 10. Characteristics of staff involved in staff sexual misconduct and harassment, by type of facility, 2006

	All facilities[a]	Prison	Jail
Gender[b]			
Male	60%	42%	79%
Female	40	58	21
Age[b]			
24 or younger	8%	9%	4%
25-29	10	14	6
30-34	13	12	14
35-39	17	17	19
40-44	24	16	34
45-54	19	24	15
55 or older	9	9	7
Race/Hispanic origin[b]			
White[c]	71%	70%	74%
Black[c]	20	24	16
Hispanic	7	5	9
Other[c,d]	2	<1	1

[a]Includes substantiated incidents reported by private prisons and jails, Indian country jails, and facilities operated by the U.S. military and ICE.

[b]Gender was reported for 558 staff; age for 532; and race/Hispanic origin for 530.

[c]Excludes staff of Hispanic origin.

[d]Includes American Indians, Alaska Natives, Asians, Native Hawaiians, and Other Pacific Islanders.

Table 11. Type and position of staff involved in staff sexual misconduct and harassment, by type of facility, 2006

	All facilities*	Prison	Jail
Type of staff involved			
Full/part-time employee	89%	80%	99%
Contract employee/vendor	10	17	2
Volunteer/intern	1	1	0
Position of staff involved			
Administrator	0%	0%	0%
Correctional officer	75	54	98
Clerical	1	2	0
Maintenance	10	17	1
Medical/health care	8	14	1
Educational	3	6	0
Other program staff	2	5	0
Other	1	2	0

Note: Detail may sum to more than 100% because more than one type of staff have been involved.

*Includes substantiated incidents reported by private prisons and jails, Indian country jails, and facilities operated by the U.S. military and ICE.

Three-quarters of staff perpetrators in 2006 lost their jobs; 56% were arrested or referred for prosecution

Correctional authorities indicated that staff had been discharged or resigned in 77% of substantiated incidents in 2006, compared to 82% in 2005 (table 12). Staff had also been arrested or referred for prosecution in 56% of incidents (compared to 45% of incidents in 2005). Approximately 10% of staff perpetrators in 2006 were disciplined, transferred or demoted, compared to 17% in 2005.

Among the multiple types of sanctions imposed on staff perpetrators during 2006, discharge or resignation was the most common, constituting 79% of incidents in prisons and 74% of those in jails. Jail staff were more likely than prison staff to be arrested or prosecuted (73% versus 43%).

Sanctions imposed on staff in substantiated incidents of staff sexual misconduct and harassment, 2005 and 2006

	2006	2005
Legal sanction	56%	45%
Arrest	24	28
Referred for prosecution	45	34
Loss of job	77	82
Other sanction	10	17

Note: Detail may sum to more than 100% because multiple response were allowed.

Half of inmates involved in staff sexual misconduct were transferred or placed in segregation

Correctional authorities indicated that the victims of staff sexual misconduct or harassment during 2006 were often transferred to another facility (31%) or placed in administrative segregation or protective custody (25%). Inmate victims had been transferred to another facility in 48% of the incidents in local jails and in 19% of the incidents in State and Federal prisons. Victims were less likely to have been moved to administrative segregation or protective custody when the incident occurred in a jail (19%) than in a prison (28%).

In most incidents of staff sexual misconduct or harassment (76%), victims received no medical followup, counseling or mental health treatment. Victims were given a medical examination in 6% of the incidents in prisons and jails. They were provided counseling or mental health treatment in 12% of the incidents.

Table 12. Impact on inmate and staff in substantiated incidents of staff sexual misconduct and harassment, 2006

	All facilities[a]	Prison	Jail
Medical followup for inmate			
Given medical examination	6%	8%	5%
Administered rape kit	10	1	18
Tested for HIV/AIDS	2	3	2
Tested for other STDs	2	3	2
Provided counseling or mental health treatment	12	17	8
None of the above	76	79	74
Any change in housing/custody for inmate			
Placed in administratve segregation or protective custody	25%	28%	19%
Placed in medical unit	1	1	0
Confined to own cell/room	3	4	2
Given a higher custody level within facility	5	5	6
Transferred to another facility	31	19	48
Other[b]	3	5	1
None of the above	46	50	42
Sanctions on staff			
Legal sanction	56%	43%	73%
Arrested	24	14	34
Referred for prosecution	45	39	57
Loss of job	77	79	74
Discharged	44	33	57
Staff resigned (prior to investigation)	26	37	13
Staff resigned (after investigation)	7	10	5
Other sanction	10	12	9
Reprimanded/disciplined	10	11	8
Demoted/diminished responsibilities	1	<1	2
Transferred to another facility	1	1	<1

Note: Detail may sum to more than 100% because multiple responses were allowed for each item.

[a]Includes substantiated incidents reported by private prisons and jails, Indian country jails, and facilities operated by the U.S. military and ICE.

[b]Includes "stayed in same unit," "transferred elsewhere in facility," and "incident reported after release."

Methodology

Measures of sexual violence

In 2004 BJS developed uniform definitions of sexual violence. All incidents of inmate-on-inmate sexual violence involve sexual contacts with any person without his or her consent, or with a person who is unable to consent or refuse. The most serious incidents, *nonconsensual sexual acts*, include:

- Contact between the penis and the vagina or the penis and the anus including penetration, however slight; or
- Contact between the mouth and the penis, vagina, or anus; or
- Penetration of the anal or genital opening of another person by a hand, finger, or other object.

The less serious incidents, *abusive sexual contacts*, include:

- Intentional touching, either directly or through the clothing, of the genitalia, anus, groin, breast, inner thigh, or buttocks of any person.
- Incidents in which the intention is to sexually exploit (rather than to only harm or debilitate).

Incidents of staff-with-inmate sexual violence are separated into two categories.

Staff sexual misconduct includes any behavior or act of a sexual nature, either consensual or nonconsensual, directed toward an inmate by an employee, volunteer, official visitor, or agency representative. Such acts include:

- Intentional touching of the genitalia, anus, groin, breast, inner thigh, or buttocks with the intent to abuse, arouse, or gratify sexual desire; or
- Completed, attempted, threatened, or requested sexual acts; or
- Occurrences of indecent exposure, invasion of privacy, or staff voyeurism for sexual gratification.

Staff sexual harassment involves repeated verbal statements or comments of a sexual nature to an inmate by an employee, volunteer, official visitor, or agency representative. Such statements include demeaning references to gender or derogatory comments about body or clothing; or profane or obscene language or gestures.

Since BJS first developed these definitions, correctional authorities have significantly enhanced their abilities to report uniform data on sexual violence. Authorities in 42 State and Federal prison systems were able to report incidents of abusive sexual contacts separately, as defined in the 2006 survey. Only two States limited reports to substantiated incidents.

Most prison systems (44) were able to report data on staff sexual misconduct using survey definitions. Five systems were unable to separate sexual harassment from misconduct. One system did not record staff sexual harassment in a central database.

Jail authorities were less likely than prison authorities to meet survey definitions. More than a third of the jail jurisdictions were unable to separate abusive sexual contacts from the more serious nonconsensual sexual acts; a quarter were unable to report staff sexual harassment separately from staff sexual misconduct.

Sampling procedures

The *2006 Survey of Sexual Violence* was based on seven separate samples, corresponding to the different facilities covered under the Act. The following samples were drawn:

1. The survey included all 50 State adult prison systems and the Federal Bureau of Prisons. Prison administrators were directed to report only on incidents of sexual violence that occurred within publicly operated adult facilities.

2. A sample of 41 privately operated prison facilities was drawn to produce a 10% sample of the 408 private prisons identified in the *2005 Census of State and Federal Adult Correctional Facilities.* Facilities were ranked by average daily population (ADP) in the 12-month period ending June 30, 2005. Four facilities with an ADP of more than 2,005 inmates were selected with certainty due to their size. The remaining facilities were sorted by region and ADP within region and then sampled systematically with a probability proportional to their size.

3. A sample of 350 publicly operated jail facilities was selected based on data reported in the *2005 Census of Jail Inmates.*

Jail jurisdictions were sorted into five strata based on ADP during the 12-month period ending June 30, 2005, and sampled systematically to produce a representative national sample. In 2006 the second-largest jail jurisdiction in each State was selected from stratum 1 to avoid selecting with certainty the same jurisdiction as in 2005. (In previous surveys the 46 largest jails in each State were selected.)

An additional 61 jail jurisdictions (forming stratum 2) were selected with certainty due to size (an ADP of 1,500 inmates or more).

The remaining 2,813 jail jurisdictions in the 2005 census were then grouped into 3 strata: stratum 3 contained 1,599 jails with an ADP of 85 inmates or fewer; stratum 4 included 785 jails with an ADP of 86 to 283 inmates; and stratum 5 included 429 jails with an ADP of 284 to 1,499 inmates. Jail jurisdictions in these 3 strata were selected systematically with probabilities proportionate to their size, resulting in 46 selections from stratum 3, 52 from stratum 4, and 145 from stratum 5.

Of the 350 selected jail jurisdictions, 5 did not respond to the survey:

Rockdale County, GA
Beaver County, PA
Lycoming County, PA
Greenville County, SC
Ellis County, TX

One of the facilities closed in 2006:

Crossville City, AL

4. A sample of 5 privately operated jails was also selected based on data reported in the *2005 Census of Jail Inmates.* The 42 private facilities were sorted by region, State, and ADP. Facilities were systematically sampled with probabilities proportionate to size.

5. Three additional samples of other correctional facilities were drawn to represent:

a) jails in Indian Country (10 facilities holding adult and juvenile inmates were selected from a total of 68 based on the ADP during 2004);

b) military-operated facilities (all 59 facilities operated by the Armed Services in the continental U.S.);

c) 14 facilities operated by Immigration and Customs Enforcement.

Of the facilities selected, one had closed (Navajo Department of Corrections – Chinle, AZ).

Data for each correctional system and sampled facility are displayed in Appendix tables 1a – 4b. In each table a measure of population size has been provided as a basis for comparison.

National estimates and accuracy

Survey responses were weighted to produce national estimates by type of correctional facility. Data from the Federal Bureau of Prisons, all State systems, military facilities, and ICE facilities received a weight of 1.00, since these systems and facilities were all selected (sampled with certainty).

Among publicly operated jails, private prisons, private jails and jails in Indian country, facilities were assigned a weight equal to the inverse of their probability of selection. Estimates for public jail jurisdictions were adjusted for nonresponse by multiplying each estimate by the ratio of the total ADP in all jurisdictions to the ADP among participating jurisdictions.

Survey estimates for public jail jurisdictions, private prisons and jails, and jails in Indian country are subject to sampling error. The error, as measured by an estimated sampling error, varies by the size of the estimate and the size of the base population. Estimates of the standard errors for selected survey items are presented in tables 13 and 14.

These standard errors may be used to construct confidence intervals around survey estimates (e.g., numbers, rates, and percentages), as well as differences in these estimates. For example, the 95% confidence interval around the number of allegations of sexual violence is approximately 6,528 plus or minus 1.96 times 143 (or 6,248 to 6,808).

Table 13. Estimated standard errors for number of allegations and substantiated incidents, by type, 2006

	Allegations		Substantiated incidents	
	National estimate	Standard error	National estimate	Standard error
Total	6,528	143	967	72
Inmate-on-inmate nonconsensual sexual acts	2,205	68	263	23
Inmate-on-inmate abusive sexual contacts	834	16	157	6
Staff sexual misconduct	2,371	106	469	68
Staff sexual harassment	1,118	41	78	8

Table 14. Estimated standard errors for selected characteristics of substantiated incidents, by type, 2006

Characteristic	National estimate	Standard error
Inmate-on-inmate sexual violence		
Occurred between 6 p.m. and midnight	45%	3%
Occurred in victim's cell	64	2
Force/threat of force used	58	3
Victim injured	20	2
Victim given medical examination	60	2
Victim placed in administrative segregation	40	2
Perpetrator placed in solitary	78	1
Legal action imposed on perpetrator	41	3
Staff-on-inmate sexual violence		
Relationship appeared to be willing	57%	6%
Occurred between 6 p.m. and midnight	56	7
Occurred in victim's cell	10	3
Victim placed in administrative segregation	25	5
Victim transferred to another facility	31	8
Legal sanction imposed on staff	56	6
Staff discharged or resigned	77	6

Detail on substantiated incidents

The 2006 Survey of Sexual Violence recorded 704 substantiated incidents of sexual violence; that is, incidents that were investigated and determined to have occurred. Taking into account sampling of local jail jurisdictions, private prisons and jails, and jails in Indian country, the estimated total for the Nation was 967.

Correctional authorities provided detail on 99% of all substantiated incidents. Through use of a separate incident form, the survey collected details on circumstances surrounding each incident, characteristics of victims and perpetrators, type of pressure or physical force, sanctions imposed, and victim assistance. These data are displayed in Appendix tables 5 – 8.

In response to concerns raised about the 2005 survey, BJS changed the survey item related to staff sexual misconduct and harassment. Item 27 of the 2006 survey read as follows:

What was the nature of the incident?

(Mark all that apply.)

1. Pressure or abuse of power resulting in a nonconsensual sexual act
2. Indecent exposure, invasion of privacy, or voyeurism for sexual gratification
3. Unwanted touching for sexual gratification
4. Sexual harassment or repeated verbal statements of a sexual nature by staff
5. Sexual relationship between inmate and staff that appeared to be willing
6. Other – *Specify*
7. Level of coercion unknown

This report in portable document format (includes 8 appendix tables) and in ASCII and its related statistical data are available at the BJS World Wide Web Internet site: <http://www.ojp.usdoj.gov/bjs/abstract/svrca06.htm>

Office of Justice Programs

Innovation • Partnerships • Safer Neighborhoods
http://www.ojp.usdoj.gov

The Bureau of Justice Statistics is the statistical agency of the U.S. Department of Justice. Jeffrey L. Sedgwick is the director.

Allen J. Beck, Paige M. Harrison and Devon B. Adams, wrote this report. Carolyn Williams produced and edited the report, and Jayne Robinson prepared the report for publication, under the supervision of Doris J. James.

Pamela H. Butler, Greta B. Clark, and Shannon Clerkin carried out data collection and processing, under the supervision of Charlene M. Sebold, Governments Division, Census Bureau, U.S. Department of Commerce. Pearl E. Chase, Patricia D. Torryson, Kathryn DiMeglio, and Lisa A. McNelis assisted in the data collection. Suzanne M. Dorinski drew the facility samples and provided sampling weights.

August 2007, NCJ 218914.

Appendix table 1a. Allegations of inmate-on-inmate sexual violence reported by State or Federal prison authorities, by type, 2006

Jurisdiction	Prisoners in custody, 6/30/2006[a]	Reported inmate-on-inmate nonconsensual sexual acts					Reported inmate-on-inmate abusive sexual contacts				
		Allegations	Substantiated	Unsubstantiated	Unfounded	Investigation ongoing	Allegations	Substantiated	Unsubstantiated	Unfounded	Investigation ongoing
Total	1,367,204	1,390	147	707	304	232	707	125	426	139	17
Federal	161,871	7	0	0	7	0	11	1	0	9	1
State	1,205,333	1,383	147	707	297	232	696	124	426	130	16
Alabama[b]	23,995	2	0	2	0	0	/	/	/	/	/
Alaska[b]	3,540	0	0	0	0	0	/	/	/	/	/
Arizona	30,391	35	0	20	12	3	4	0	2	2	0
Arkansas	12,643	10	4	0	6	0	5	0	0	5	0
California	169,561	76	5	41	17	13	8	3	5	0	0
Colorado	17,204	28	5	17	5	1	15	2	11	2	0
Connecticut	19,606	19	0	14	0	5	3	0	0	3	0
Delaware	7,090	6	2	2	2	0	0	0	0	0	0
Florida	82,223	145	1	140	1	3	22	0	22	0	0
Georgia[b]	46,359	53	2	14	1	36	/	/	/	/	/
Hawaii	3,898	1	0	0	0	1	0	0	0	0	0
Idaho	4,735	17	9	5	3	0	17	10	6	1	0
Illinois	45,440	38	4	30	0	4	0	0	0	0	0
Indiana	22,539	29	0	23	6	0	15	3	8	4	0
Iowa	8,659	20	2	10	8	0	34	13	14	7	0
Kansas	8,952	47	4	21	21	1	13	0	3	10	0
Kentucky	12,967	10	1	7	2	0	6	1	5	0	0
Louisiana	17,387	24	3	5	16	0	2	2	0	0	0
Maine	2,028	0	0	0	0	0	0	0	0	0	0
Maryland	22,860	15	2	6	1	6	1	0	0	1	0
Massachusetts	10,683	22	7	7	8	0	32	8	16	8	0
Michigan	50,701	33	10	23	0	0	18	18	0	0	0
Minnesota	8,017	22	0	4	17	1	5	1	2	2	0
Mississippi[b]	11,528	1	0	0	1	0	/	/	/	/	/
Missouri	30,149	49	2	28	18	1	15	2	7	6	0
Montana[c]	1,968	12	3	7	2	0	4	2	1	1	0
Nebraska	4,546	7	2	4	1	0	7	2	4	1	0
Nevada[b]	12,412	21	0	7	8	6	/	/	/	/	/
New Hampshire	2,522	8	7	0	1	0	1	1	0	0	0
New Jersey	23,987	2	0	2	0	0	1	0	1	0	0
New Mexico	3,876	0	0	0	0	0	0	0	0	0	0
New York	63,479	34	1	22	0	11	16	4	5	0	7
North Carolina[b]	37,277	22	4	16	2	0	/	/	/	/	/
North Dakota	1,370	2	1	1	0	0	5	3	2	0	0
Ohio	44,759	67	16	5	45	1	34	9	5	20	0
Oklahoma	17,149	17	2	7	8	0	0	0	0	0	0
Oregon	13,091	23	0	4	2	17	2	0	2	0	0
Pennsylvania	41,957	24	5	5	14	0	1	1	0	0	0
Rhode Island	3,645	9	3	4	2	0	3	1	1	1	0
South Carolina[d]	22,898	2	2	0	0	0	0	0	0	0	0
South Dakota	3,573	1	0	0	0	1	3	1	0	2	0
Tennessee	14,235	17	0	14	2	1	7	1	4	2	0
Texas	140,166	297	4	136	45	112	349	19	279	43	8
Utah	4,978	15	4	11	0	0	15	1	12	2	0
Vermont	1,678	12	6	3	1	2	18	9	5	3	1
Virginia[b]	29,539	16	1	2	8	5	/	/	/	/	/
Washington	15,289	26	4	19	3	0	7	3	3	1	0
West Virginia[d]	4,276	1	1	0	0	0	0	0	0	0	0
Wisconsin[b]	22,279	40	17	17	6	0	/	/	/	/	/
Wyoming	1,229	6	1	2	2	1	8	4	1	3	0

/Not reported

[a]Excludes inmates in private facilities. Counts were based on National Prisoners Statistics (NPS-1A), 2006.

[b]Allegations of abusive sexual contacts could not be counted separately from allegations of nonconsensual sexual acts.

[c]Includes consensual sexual acts between inmates.

[d]Allegations limited to substantiated occurrences only.

Appendix table 1b. Allegations of staff-on-inmate sexual violence reported by State or Federal prison authorities, by type, 2006

	Reported allegations of staff sexual misconduct with inmates					Reported allegations of staff sexual harassment of inmates				
Jurisdiction	Allegations	Substanti-ated	Unsubstan-tiated	Unfounded	Investigation ongoing	Allegations	Substanti-ated	Unsubstan-tiated	Unfounded	Investigation ongoing
Total	1,677	235	745	309	388	984	47	537	258	142
Federal	133	4	50	0	79	91	0	46	0	45
State	1,544	231	695	309	309	893	47	491	258	97
Alabama	4	1	3	0	0	3	0	3	0	0
Alaska	0	0	0	0	0	0	0	0	0	0
Arizona	26	8	10	6	2	8	0	4	3	1
Arkansas	7	4	0	3	0	19	0	4	15	0
California	52	11	15	14	12	30	2	11	6	11
Colorado	44	8	6	23	7	8	1	1	5	1
Connecticut	12	1	9	0	2	0	0	0	0	0
Delaware	2	0	2	0	0	2	0	2	0	0
Florida	152	0	131	10	11	144	0	133	4	7
Georgia	133	6	26	0	101	73	6	21	0	46
Hawaii	0	0	0	0	0	1	0	0	0	1
Idaho	14	7	5	2	0	3	1	2	0	0
Illinois	23	11	9	0	3	0	0	0	0	0
Indiana	32	7	16	9	0	8	2	4	2	0
Iowa	48	11	15	21	1	39	7	13	19	0
Kansas	41	4	30	7	0	4	1	3	0	0
Kentucky	7	5	1	1	0	0	0	0	0	0
Louisiana	71	9	42	18	2	66	0	31	29	6
Maine	2	0	1	1	0	2	1	0	1	0
Maryland	17	0	6	5	6	1	0	1	0	0
Massachusetts	61	7	6	17	31	11	1	5	4	1
Michigan	27	2	8	16	1	337	4	179	143	11
Minnesota	15	2	6	5	2	0	0	0	0	0
Mississippi	5	2	1	2	0	0	0	0	0	0
Missouri	73	7	24	40	2	21	2	15	4	0
Montana	2	1	0	1	0	2	2	0	0	0
Nebraska	13	2	2	9	0	2	1	1	0	0
Nevada[a]	11	1	6	1	3	/	/	/	/	/
New Hampshire	3	1	1	1	0	1	0	1	0	0
New Jersey[a]	2	0	0	0	2	/	/	/	/	/
New Mexico[a]	0	0	0	0	0	/	/	/	/	/
New York	209	19	119	0	71	34	2	25	0	7
North Carolina[a]	9	8	1	0	0	/	/	/	/	/
North Dakota	3	0	1	2	0	2	0	0	2	0
Ohio	89	4	78	6	1	21	0	19	0	2
Oklahoma	25	7	15	2	1	2	0	2	0	0
Oregon	14	3	4	2	5	8	1	1	6	0
Pennsylvania	24	7	5	12	0	6	0	0	6	0
Rhode Island[a]	2	0	0	2	0	/	/	/	/	/
South Carolina	0	0	0	0	0	0	0	0	0	0
South Dakota	3	2	0	0	1	2	0	0	2	0
Tennessee	14	8	4	0	2	7	2	4	1	0
Texas[b]	79	10	28	10	31	/	/	/	/	/
Utah	6	0	5	1	0	2	1	1	0	0
Vermont	20	10	5	5	0	8	4	0	2	2
Virginia	39	13	2	17	7	3	1	0	1	1
Washington	34	5	24	5	0	2	1	0	1	0
West Virginia	7	6	0	1	0	0	0	0	0	0
Wisconsin	53	6	20	27	0	9	2	5	2	0
Wyoming	15	5	3	5	2	2	2	0	0	0

/Not reported

[a]Reports of staff sexual misconduct may include reports of staff sexual harassment.

[b]Reports of staff sexual harassment are not recorded in a central database.

Appendix table 2a. Allegations of inmate-on-inmate sexual violence reported by local jail authorities, by type, 2006

Jurisdiction and facility	Average daily population, 2006	Reported inmate-on-inmate nonconsensual sexual acts					Reported inmate-on-inmate abusive sexual contacts				
		Allega-tions	Substan-tiated	Unsub-stantiated	Unfounded	Investiga-tion ongoing	Allega-tions	Substan-tiated	Unsub-stantiated	Unfounded	Investiga-tion ongoing
Total	380,894	403	52	192	123	36	73	19	38	14	2
Alabama											
Butler County	36	0	0	0	0	0	0	0	0	0	0
Calhoun County[a]	370	0	0	0	0	0	/	/	/	/	/
Cullman County[a]	194	0	0	0	0	0	/	/	/	/	/
Etowah County	800	0	0	0	0	0	0	0	0	0	0
Jefferson County[a]	964	5	3	1	1	0	/	/	/	/	/
Shelby County	503	0	0	0	0	0	0	0	0	0	0
Talledega County[a]	226	0	0	0	0	0	/	/	/	/	/
Tarrant City	9	0	0	0	0	0	0	0	0	0	0
Alaska											
Seward County	8	0	0	0	0	0	0	0	0	0	0
Kodiak City	10	0	0	0	0	0	0	0	0	0	0
Arizona											
Coconino County	509	0	0	0	0	0	0	0	0	0	0
Maricopa County[a]	9,247	16	4	6	4	2	/	/	/	/	/
Navajo County	354	0	0	0	0	0	0	0	0	0	0
Pima County	1,858	1	0	0	1	0	0	0	0	0	0
Arkansas											
Arkansas County[a]	109	0	0	0	0	0	/	/	/	/	/
Johnson County[a]	29	0	0	0	0	0	/	/	/	/	/
Sebastian County	322	0	0	0	0	0	0	0	0	0	0
Siloam Springs City[a,b]	5	0	0	0	0	0	/	/	/	/	/
Washington County[a,b,c]	501	0	0	0	0	0	/	/	/	/	/
California											
Alameda County	4,020	8	4	3	1	0	1	1	0	0	0
Contra Costa County	1,663	1	1	0	0	0	0	0	0	0	0
El Dorado County	363	0	0	0	0	0	0	0	0	0	0
Fresno County[a]	3,024	0	0	0	0	0	/	/	/	/	/
Kern County	2,324	0	0	0	0	0	1	0	1	0	0
Los Angeles County[a]	19,011	44	1	43	0	0	/	/	/	/	/
Orange County	6,157	3	0	3	0	0	0	0	0	0	0
Riverside County	3,287	1	1	0	0	0	1	1	0	0	0
Sacramento County[a]	2,121	2	2	0	0	0	/	/	/	/	/
San Bernardino County West Valley[a,b,c,d]	5,567	0	0	0	0	0	/	/	/	/	/
San Diego County	5,168	6	0	2	1	3	6	1	3	1	1
San Francisco City[a]	1,915	7	0	5	2	0	/	/	/	/	/
San Joaquin County[a]	1,431	1	0	1	0	0	/	/	/	/	/
San Luis Obispo County[a]	531	0	0	0	0	0	/	/	/	/	/
San Mateo County	1,124	0	0	0	0	0	0	0	0	0	0
Santa Barbara County	980	0	0	0	0	0	0	0	0	0	0
Santa Clara County	4,471	2	0	2	0	0	2	0	2	0	0
Santa Clara County Mountain View	184	0	0	0	0	0	0	0	0	0	0
Santa Cruz County[a]	537	0	0	0	0	0	/	/	/	/	/
Ventura County	1,651	0	0	0	0	0	0	0	0	0	0
Yuba County	419	0	0	0	0	0	0	0	0	0	0
Colorado											
Arapahoe County	1,335	2	1	1	0	0	0	0	0	0	0
Boulder County	470	1	1	0	0	0	0	0	0	0	0
Denver County	2,475	9	0	4	5	0	1	0	1	0	0
El Paso County	1,433	2	0	1	1	0	0	0	0	0	0
Logan County	120	0	0	0	0	0	0	0	0	0	0
Pueblo County[a]	526	4	0	1	0	3	/	/	/	/	/
Rio Grande County[a]	32	0	0	0	0	0	/	/	/	/	/
District of Columbia											
District of Columbia	3,473	2	0	0	2	0	0	0	0	0	0

Appendix table 2a. Allegations of inmate-on-inmate sexual violence reported by local jail authorities, by type, 2006 (cont).										
	Average daily population, 2006	Reported inmate-on-inmate nonconsensual sexual acts					Reported inmate-on-inmate abusive sexual contacts				
Jurisdiction and facility		Allegations	Substantiated	Unsubstantiated	Unfounded	Investigation ongoing	Allegations	Substantiated	Unsubstantiated	Unfounded	Investigation ongoing
Florida											
Alachua County[a]	1,065	8	0	2	6	0	/	/	/	/	/
Broward County[a]	5,662	12	0	9	3	0	/	/	/	/	/
Escambia County	1,908	1	1	0	0	0	0	0	0	0	0
Highlands County	386	0	0	0	0	0	0	0	0	0	0
Hillsborough County[a]	4,637	4	0	4	0	0	/	/	/	/	/
Indian River County[a]	559	6	0	0	6	0	/	/	/	/	/
Jackson County	233	0	0	0	0	0	0	0	0	0	0
Jacksonville City	3,629	0	0	0	0	0	8	0	5	3	0
Lee County[c]	1,899	3	1	1	1	0	0	0	0	0	0
Manatee County	1,466	1	0	1	0	0	1	0	1	0	0
Marion County[a]	1,881	3	0	2	0	1	/	/	/	/	/
Martin County	595	0	0	0	0	0	1	1	0	0	0
Miami-Dade County[a]	6,686	1	1	0	0	0	/	/	/	/	/
Orange County[a]	4,104	0	0	0	0	0	/	/	/	/	/
Palm Beach County[a]	1,902	3	1	0	2	0	/	/	/	/	/
Pinellas County[a]	3,630	0	0	0	0	0	/	/	/	/	/
Polk County	2,523	6	0	4	0	2	2	0	2	0	0
St Lucie County	1,349	1	0	1	0	0	1	1	0	0	0
Seminole County	1,017	3	0	3	0	0	0	0	0	0	0
Taylor County	84	0	0	0	0	0	0	0	0	0	0
Volusia County	1,536	1	1	0	0	0	2	2	0	0	0
Georgia											
Atlanta City	1,079	0	0	0	0	0	0	0	0	0	0
Bibb County	637	1	0	1	0	0	0	0	0	0	0
Carroll County Corr. Inst.	525	1	1	0	0	0	0	0	0	0	0
Carroll County	513	1	1	0	0	0	0	0	0	0	0
Chatham County[a]	1,622	1	0	1	0	0	/	/	/	/	/
Clayton County[e]	1,585	0	0	0	0	0	/	/	/	/	/
Clinch County	20	0	0	0	0	0	0	0	0	0	0
Cobb County	2,042	0	0	0	0	0	2	0	1	1	0
DeKalb County[a]	2,849	4	2	2	0	0	/	/	/	/	/
Dougherty County	876	0	0	0	0	0	0	0	0	0	0
Fulton County	143	0	0	0	0	0	0	0	0	0	0
Glynn County[a]	428	0	0	0	0	0	/	/	/	/	/
Gwinnett County[a]	2,280	0	0	0	0	0	/	/	/	/	/
Houston County	420	0	0	0	0	0	0	0	0	0	0
Jackson County[a]	172	0	0	0	0	0	/	/	/	/	/
Lamar County[a]	135	0	0	0	0	0	/	/	/	/	/
Lee County	69	0	0	0	0	0	0	0	0	0	0
Murray County[a]	106	0	0	0	0	0	/	/	/	/	/
Muscogee County[a]	588	0	0	0	0	0	/	/	/	/	/
Newton County[c]	553	0	0	0	0	0	0	0	0	0	0
Rockdale County	*	*	*	*	*	*	*	*	*	*	*
Spalding County	461	1	1	0	0	0	0	0	0	0	0
Idaho											
Benewah County	19	0	0	0	0	0	0	0	0	0	0
Canyon County	683	0	0	0	0	0	0	0	0	0	0
Kootenai County[a]	370	0	0	0	0	0	/	/	/	/	/
Illinois											
Champaign County[a]	213	0	0	0	0	0	/	/	/	/	/
Cook County[a]	9,359	12	2	3	3	4	/	/	/	/	/
Du Page County	824	0	0	0	0	0	1	1	0	0	0
Lake County[a]	603	0	0	0	0	0	/	/	/	/	/
McLean County	230	0	0	0	0	0	0	0	0	0	0
St Clair County[a,b]	427	0	0	0	0	0	/	/	/	/	/
Schuyler County[a,b,c]	27	0	0	0	0	0	/	/	/	/	/
Whiteside County	98	0	0	0	0	0	0	0	0	0	0

Appendix table 2a. Allegations of inmate-on-inmate sexual violence reported by local jail authorities, by type, 2006 (cont.)

Jurisdiction and facility	Average daily population, 2006	Reported inmate-on-inmate nonconsensual sexual acts					Reported inmate-on-inmate abusive sexual contacts				
		Allegations	Substantiated	Unsubstantiated	Unfounded	Investigation ongoing	Allegations	Substantiated	Unsubstantiated	Unfounded	Investigation ongoing
Indiana											
Allen County	736	2	0	2	0	0	0	0	0	0	0
Howard County	378	0	0	0	0	0	/	/	/	/	/
Kosciusko County[a]	186	0	0	0	0	0	/	/	/	/	/
Lake County	902	3	0	3	0	0	0	0	0	0	0
La Porte County	275	0	0	0	0	0	0	0	0	0	0
Marion County	334	0	0	0	0	0	0	0	0	0	0
Montgomery County	144	0	0	0	0	0	0	0	0	0	0
Porter County	468	1	0	1	0	0	0	0	0	0	0
Pulaski County[a,c]	2	0	0	0	0	0	/	/	/	/	/
Union County	22	0	0	0	0	0	0	0	0	0	0
Iowa											
Adams County	6	0	0	0	0	0	0	0	0	0	0
Dubuque County[a]	116	0	0	0	0	0	/	/	/	/	/
Jasper County	60	0	0	0	0	0	0	0	0	0	0
Linn County[a]	389	0	0	0	0	0	/	/	/	/	/
Kansas											
Crawford County	97	0	0	0	0	0	0	0	0	0	0
Graham County[e,f]	7	/	/	/	/	/	/	/	/	/	/
Johnson County	880	0	0	0	0	0	0	0	0	0	0
Meade County	29	0	0	0	0	0	0	0	0	0	0
Shawnee County	435	1	0	0	1	0	1	0	0	1	0
Kentucky											
Calloway County[b]	172	0	0	0	0	0	0	0	0	0	0
Estill County	26	0	0	0	0	0	0	0	0	0	0
Franklin County	308	0	0	0	0	0	1	0	0	1	0
Kenton County	428	1	0	1	0	0	0	0	0	0	0
Laurel County	327	0	0	0	0	0	1	1	0	0	0
Lexington-Fayette County	1,220	0	0	0	0	0	0	0	0	0	0
Louisville Metropolitan Dept. of Corr.[a]	2,000	3	0	0	3	0	/	/	/	/	/
Pulaski County[a,d]	256	0	0	0	0	0	/	/	/	/	/
Rockcastle County	82	0	0	0	0	0	0	0	0	0	0
Warren County	565	0	0	0	0	0	0	0	0	0	0
Louisiana											
Bayou Dorcheat Corr. Ctr.[a,c]	481	0	0	0	0	0	/	/	/	/	/
East Baton Rouge Prison	1,778	0	0	0	0	0	1	0	1	0	0
Grant Parish	103	0	0	0	0	0	0	0	0	0	0
Jefferson Parish[a]	738	0	0	0	0	0	/	/	/	/	/
Madison Corr. Ctr.[a,b]	600	1	0	1	0	0	/	/	/	/	/
Ouachita Parish	25	1	0	1	0	0	0	0	0	0	0
New Orleans Parish[a]	1,896	7	3	4	0	0	/	/	/	/	/
St. Charles Parish[a]	552	0	0	0	0	0	/	/	/	/	/
St. Tammany Parish[a,b]	687	0	0	0	0	0	/	/	/	/	/
Tangipahoa Parish	520	0	0	0	0	0	0	0	0	0	0
Union Parish[a]	313	0	0	0	0	0	/	/	/	/	/
Vermilion Parish	146	0	0	0	0	0	0	0	0	0	0
Terrebonne Parish[a]	636	1	0	0	1	0	/	/	/	/	/
Maine											
Cumberland County	474	0	0	0	0	0	0	0	0	0	0
York County[a]	187	0	0	0	0	0	/	/	/	/	/
Maryland											
Allegany County	167	0	0	0	0	0	0	0	0	0	0
Baltimore City	3,708	2	0	0	0	2	0	0	0	0	0
Baltimore County[a]	1,290	1	0	1	0	0	/	/	/	/	/
Frederick County[a]	496	2	0	2	0	0	/	/	/	/	/
Prince Georges County	1,439	2	0	1	1	0	0	0	0	0	0
Washington County	391	2	1	0	1	0	0	0	0	0	0
Worcester County[a]	223	0	0	0	0	0	/	/	/	/	/

Appendix table 2a. Allegations of inmate-on-inmate sexual violence reported by local jail authorities, by type, 2006 (cont.)

Jurisdiction and facility	Average daily population, 2006	Reported inmate-on-inmate nonconsensual sexual acts					Reported inmate-on-inmate abusive sexual contacts				
		Allegations	Substantiated	Unsubstantiated	Unfounded	Investigation ongoing	Allegations	Substantiated	Unsubstantiated	Unfounded	Investigation ongoing
Massachusetts											
Berkshire County	257	0	0	0	0	0	0	0	0	0	0
Essex County[a]	1,167	1	0	0	1	0	/	/	/	/	/
Hampden County[a]	2,017	5	0	5	0	0	/	/	/	/	/
Plymouth County	1,598	0	0	0	0	0	0	0	0	0	0
Suffolk County	1,760	2	0	0	2	0	2	0	2	0	0
Worcester County	1,397	0	0	0	0	0	0	0	0	0	0
Michigan											
Allegan County	163	0	0	0	0	0	0	0	0	0	0
Genesee County[a]	638	1	0	1	0	0	/	/	/	/	/
Gogebic County	26	0	0	0	0	0	0	0	0	0	0
Jackson County	409	0	0	0	0	0	0	0	0	0	0
Macomb County	1,348	0	0	0	0	0	3	0	2	1	0
Monroe County	367	0	0	0	0	0	0	0	0	0	0
Oakland County	1,973	1	0	0	1	0	0	0	0	0	0
Ottawa County	369	0	0	0	0	0	1	1	0	0	0
Wayne County[a]	3,005	0	0	0	0	0	/	/	/	/	/
Minnesota											
Hennepin County	586	0	0	0	0	0	0	0	0	0	0
Mille Lacs County	71	0	0	0	0	0	0	0	0	0	0
Pipestone County	11	0	0	0	0	0	0	0	0	0	0
Sherburne County[b,c]	510	0	0	0	0	0	0	0	0	0	0
Washington County	203	0	0	0	0	0	0	0	0	0	0
Mississippi											
Adams County	80	0	0	0	0	0	0	0	0	0	0
Desoto County	368	0	0	0	0	0	0	0	0	0	0
Harrison County[a]	815	4	2	2	0	0	/	/	/	/	/
Hinds County[a]	925	0	0	0	0	0	/	/	/	/	/
Humphreys County	27	0	0	0	0	0	0	0	0	0	0
Issaquena County[a,c]	4	0	0	0	0	0	/	/	/	/	/
Kemper-Neshoda County Reg. Corr. Fac.[e]	283	0	0	0	0	0	0	0	0	0	0
Leake County	345	0	0	0	0	0	0	0	0	0	0
Winston/Chocktaw Reg. Corr. Fac.	76	0	0	0	0	0	0	0	0	0	0
Missouri											
Cass County[a]	108	1	0	0	1	0	/	/	/	/	/
Howard County[a]	11	0	0	0	0	0	/	/	/	/	/
Lincoln County	152	0	0	0	0	0	0	0	0	0	0
St Charles County	282	0	0	0	0	0	0	0	0	0	0
St. Louis City	1,727	0	0	0	0	0	0	0	0	0	0
St. Louis County	993	0	0	0	0	0	0	0	0	0	0
Taney County[a]	69	0	0	0	0	0	/	/	/	/	/
Vernon County	24	0	0	0	0	0	0	0	0	0	0
Montana											
Anaconda-Deer Lodge County[a]	26	0	0	0	0	0	/	/	/	/	/
Cascade County	427	0	0	0	0	0	0	0	0	0	0
Yellowstone County[a,b]	409	0	0	0	0	0	/	/	/	/	/
Nebraska											
Clay County	7	0	0	0	0	0	0	0	0	0	0
Douglas County	976	4	0	2	1	1	3	0	3	0	0
Lancaster County	429	0	0	0	0	0	1	1	0	0	0
Nevada											
Clark County	3,540	0	0	0	0	0	2	0	1	1	0
Las Vegas City[a,d]	1,119	1	0	0	1	0	/	/	/	/	/
Washoe County	1,137	6	2	0	4	0	4	0	2	2	0
New Hampshire											
Rockingham County	338	0	0	0	0	0	0	0	0	0	0

Appendix table 2a. Allegations of inmate-on-inmate sexual violence reported by local jail authorities, by type, 2006 (cont.)

Jurisdiction and facility	Average daily population, 2006	Reported inmate-on-inmate nonconsensual sexual acts					Reported inmate-on-inmate abusive sexual contacts				
		Allegations	Substantiated	Unsubstantiated	Unfounded	Investigation ongoing	Allegations	Substantiated	Unsubstantiated	Unfounded	Investigation ongoing
New Jersey											
Atlantic County	1,358	0	0	0	0	0	0	0	0	0	0
Camden County	1,646	3	0	2	1	0	0	0	0	0	0
Cape May County	279	2	0	2	0	0	0	0	0	0	0
Cumberland County[d]	575	2	0	1	1	0	0	0	0	0	0
Essex County	2,081	0	0	0	0	0	0	0	0	0	0
Gloucester County	358	0	0	0	0	0	0	0	0	0	0
Hudson County[a]	2,008	11	1	5	3	2	/	/	/	/	/
Passaic County[a]	1,946	1	0	0	1	0	/	/	/	/	/
Union County	1,122	1	1	0	0	0	0	0	0	0	0
New Mexico											
Bernalillo County[a]	2,377	4	1	2	0	1	/	/	/	/	/
Dona Ana County[a]	890	0	0	0	0	0	/	/	/	/	/
Luna County[a]	394	0	0	0	0	0	/	/	/	/	/
Otero County	242	1	1	0	0	0	0	0	0	0	0
Quay County[a]	80	0	0	0	0	0	/	/	/	/	/
New York											
Albany County	832	0	0	0	0	0	0	0	0	0	0
Allegany County[a,b]	53	0	0	0	0	0	/	/	/	/	/
Broome County	527	0	0	0	0	0	0	0	0	0	0
Dutchess County	309	0	0	0	0	0	0	0	0	0	0
Erie County[a]	925	0	0	0	0	0	/	/	/	/	/
Montgomery County	119	0	0	0	0	0	0	0	0	0	0
Nassau County[c]	1,633	1	0	1	0	0	0	0	0	0	0
New York City[a]	13,788	13	0	5	6	2	/	/	/	/	/
Suffolk County[a]	1,632	0	0	0	0	0	/	/	/	/	/
North Carolina											
Buncombe County	458	0	0	0	0	0	0	0	0	0	0
Cabarrus County	230	0	0	0	0	0	0	0	0	0	0
Carteret County[d]	122	0	0	0	0	0	0	0	0	0	0
Cumberland County	532	1	1	0	0	0	0	0	0	0	0
Gaston County	526	0	0	0	0	0	0	0	0	0	0
Mecklenburg County	2,484	2	0	0	1	1	0	0	0	0	0
Rockingham County	165	1	0	0	1	0	0	0	0	0	0
Swain County	44	0	0	0	0	0	0	0	0	0	0
Wake County	1,240	0	0	0	0	0	0	0	0	0	0
North Dakota											
Burleigh County	115	0	0	0	0	0	0	0	0	0	0
Rolette County	13	0	0	0	0	0	0	0	0	0	0
Ohio											
Cuyahoga County	2,066	3	1	0	2	0	1	1	0	0	0
Franklin County[a]	2,377	1	0	1	0	0	/	/	/	/	/
Greene County	380	0	0	0	0	0	0	0	0	0	0
Hamilton County	2,157	1	1	0	0	0	3	3	0	0	0
Logan County[a]	108	0	0	0	0	0	/	/	/	/	/
Lorain County	476	3	0	1	2	0	0	0	0	0	0
Montgomery County[a]	904	1	1	0	0	0	/	/	/	/	/
Noble County	15	0	0	0	0	0	0	0	0	0	0
Northwest Ohio Reg. Corr. Ctr.[a]	581	4	0	4	0	0	/	/	/	/	/
Richland County	131	0	0	0	0	0	0	0	0	0	0
Warren County[a]	193	1	0	0	1	0	/	/	/	/	/
Oklahoma											
Garfield County[a]	182	0	0	0	0	0	/	/	/	/	/
Grady County[f]	324	0	0	0	0	0	0	0	0	0	0
Harmon County[e,f]	7	/	/	/	/	/	/	/	/	/	/
Oklahoma County	2,859	0	0	0	0	0	4	0	4	0	0
Pawnee County[a]	9	0	0	0	0	0	/	/	/	/	/
Oregon											
Marion County	540	0	0	0	0	0	0	0	0	0	0
Multnomah County	1,673	5	1	4	0	0	0	0	0	0	0
Northern Oregon Reg. Fac.	169	0	0	0	0	0	0	0	0	0	0
Washington County	554	0	0	0	0	0	0	0	0	0	0

Appendix table 2a. Allegations of inmate-on-inmate sexual violence reported by local jail authorities, by type, 2006 (cont.)

Jurisdiction and facility	Average daily population, 2006	Reported inmate-on-inmate nonconsensual sexual acts					Reported inmate-on-inmate abusive sexual contacts				
		Allegations	Substantiated	Unsubstantiated	Unfounded	Investigation ongoing	Allegations	Substantiated	Unsubstantiated	Unfounded	Investigation ongoing
Pennsylvania											
Allegheny County[a]	2,584	2	0	2	0	0	/	/	/	/	/
Beaver County	*	*	*	*	*	*	*	*	*	*	*
Berks County	1,324	2	1	0	1	0	1	1	0	0	0
Bucks County	987	2	0	1	1	0	1	1	0	0	0
Clinton County[a]	332	0	0	0	0	0	/	/	/	/	/
Erie County	740	0	0	0	0	0	0	0	0	0	0
Lycoming County	*	*	*	*	*	*	*	*	*	*	*
Philadelphia Prison System	8,603	11	0	7	0	4	1	0	0	0	1
Schuykill County[a]	270	0	0	0	0	0	/	/	/	/	/
Warren County	120	0	0	0	0	0	0	0	0	0	0
Westmoreland County	598	0	0	0	0	0	0	0	0	0	0
York County[a,c]	2,031	0	0	0	0	0	/	/	/	/	/
South Carolina											
Anderson County	433	0	0	0	0	0	0	0	0	0	0
Charleston County[a]	1,722	4	0	0	3	1	/	/	/	/	/
Cherokee County	160	0	0	0	0	0	0	0	0	0	0
Greenville County	*	*	*	*	*	*	*	*	*	*	*
Marlboro County	71	0	0	0	0	0	0	0	0	0	0
Spartanburg County[a]	808	0	0	0	0	0	/	/	/	/	/
Sumter-Lee Reg. Det. Ctr.	430	0	0	0	0	0	0	0	0	0	0
South Dakota											
Charles Mix County	6	0	0	0	0	0	0	0	0	0	0
Pennington County	421	1	0	0	1	0	2	1	0	1	0
Tennessee											
Blount County[a]	347	0	0	0	0	0	/	/	/	/	/
Cheatham County[d]	95	0	0	0	0	0	0	0	0	0	0
Clay County[a]	12	0	0	0	0	0	/	/	/	/	/
Davidson County	2,297	9	0	4	4	1	0	0	0	0	0
Madison County	331	0	0	0	0	0	0	0	0	0	0
Marion County	80	0	0	0	0	0	0	0	0	0	0
McMinn County[b,c,d]	188	0	0	0	0	0	0	0	0	0	0
She by County Corr. Ctr.	2,288	0	0	0	0	0	0	0	0	0	0
She by County Justice Ctr.[a]	2,741	2	0	0	2	0	/	/	/	/	/
Sullivan County	588	1	0	1	0	0	0	0	0	0	0
Washington County	500	0	0	0	0	0	0	0	0	0	0
Texas											
Bell County	689	1	0	0	1	0	0	0	0	0	0
Bexar County[a]	4,027	0	0	0	0	0	/	/	/	/	/
Culberson County	13	0	0	0	0	0	0	0	0	0	0
Dallas County[a]	6,324	2	0	0	2	0	/	/	/	/	/
Denton County[a]	1,020	0	0	0	0	0	/	/	/	/	/
Ector County	529	0	0	0	0	0	0	0	0	0	0
Ellis County	*	*	*	*	*	*	*	*	*	*	*
El Paso County[a]	2,090	0	0	0	0	0	/	/	/	/	/
Harris County	9,249	17	0	5	8	4	6	1	5	0	0
Hays County[a,b]	315	0	0	0	0	0	/	/	/	/	/
Hidalgo County[b]	1,128	0	0	0	0	0	0	0	0	0	0
Live Oak County	23	0	0	0	0	0	0	0	0	0	0
McLennan County	860	1	0	0	1	0	1	0	0	1	0
Milam County[a]	95	0	0	0	0	0	/	/	/	/	/
Montgomery County	1,067	1	0	1	0	0	0	0	0	0	0
Orange County[a]	214	0	0	0	0	0	/	/	/	/	/
Rusk County[a]	86	0	0	0	0	0	/	/	/	/	/
Tarrant County	3,356	0	0	0	0	0	0	0	0	0	0
Tom Green County[a]	514	0	0	0	0	0	/	/	/	/	/
Travis County	2,584	4	0	0	3	1	2	0	2	0	0
Walker County	150	0	0	0	0	0	0	0	0	0	0
Webb County[a]	681	0	0	0	0	0	/	/	/	/	/
Wharton County[a]	130	0	0	0	0	0	/	/	/	/	/
Wichita County[a]	495	0	0	0	0	0	/	/	/	/	/

Appendix table 2a. Allegations of inmate-on-inmate sexual violence reported by local jail authorities, by type, 2006 (cont.)

Jurisdiction and facility	Average daily popu-lation, 2006	Reported inmate-on-inmate nonconsensual sexual acts					Reported inmate-on-inmate abusive sexual contacts				
		Allega-tions	Substan-tiated	Unsub-stantiated	Unfounded	Investiga-tion ongoing	Allega-tions	Substan-tiated	Unsub-stantiated	Unfounded	Investiga-tion ongoing
Utah											
Daggett County	92	0	0	0	0	0	0	0	0	0	0
Davis County	500	0	0	0	0	0	0	0	0	0	0
Salt Lake County[a]	1,963	2	0	1	1	0	/	/	/	/	/
Weber County[a]	1,024	0	0	0	0	0	/	/	/	/	/
Virginia											
Abingdon Reg. Jail Fac.	383	1	0	0	1	0	0	0	0	0	0
Augusta County	230	0	0	0	0	0	0	0	0	0	0
Blue Ridge Reg. Jail Auth.	1,170	0	0	0	0	0	0	0	0	0	0
Gloucester County	75	0	0	0	0	0	0	0	0	0	0
Middle River Reg. Jail	517	0	0	0	0	0	0	0	0	0	0
New River Valley Reg. Jail[a]	630	4	0	3	1	0	/	/	/	/	/
Norfo k City	1,733	4	0	0	4	0	0	0	0	0	0
Northern Neck Reg. Jail	423	0	0	0	0	0	0	0	0	0	0
Peumansend Creek Reg. Jail[a]	295	0	0	0	0	0	/	/	/	/	/
Portsmouth City	557	0	0	0	0	0	0	0	0	0	0
Prince William-Manassas Reg. Adult Corr. Ctr.[a]	721	0	0	0	0	0	/	/	/	/	/
Richmond City	1,564	2	0	1	1	0	0	0	0	0	0
Riverside Reg. Jail	1,096	0	0	0	0	0	0	0	0	0	0
Virginia Beach Municipal[a]	1,501	2	0	2	0	0	/	/	/	/	/
Washington											
Clark County	790	1	1	0	0	0	0	0	0	0	0
Cowlitz County	277	1	0	0	0	1	0	0	0	0	0
Issaquah County	54	0	0	0	0	0	0	0	0	0	0
King County[a]	2,666	3	0	2	1	0	/	/	/	/	/
Pierce County[a]	1,359	0	0	0	0	0	/	/	/	/	/
Spokane County	569	0	0	0	0	0	0	0	0	0	0
Whatcom County	358	0	0	0	0	0	1	0	0	1	0
West Virginia											
Eastern Reg. Jail	386	0	0	0	0	0	0	0	0	0	0
Marshall County North-ern Reg. Jail & Corr. Complex	323	1	1	0	0	0	0	0	0	0	0
North Central Reg. Jail[a]	524	11	0	0	11	0	/	/	/	/	/
Raleigh County Southern Reg. Jail[a]	521	0	0	0	0	0	/	/	/	/	/
Wisconsin											
Dane County[g]	931	/	/	/	/	/	/	/	/	/	/
Jefferson County[c]	183	0	0	0	0	0	0	0	0	0	0
Milwaukee County	886	0	0	0	0	0	0	0	0	0	0
Milwaukee County House of Corr.[a]	2,331	2	2	0	0	0	/	/	/	/	/
Outagamie County[e]	460	0	0	0	0	0	/	/	/	/	/
Racine County	683	0	0	0	0	0	0	0	0	0	0
Vernon County	49	0	0	0	0	0	0	0	0	0	0
Walworth County[a]	343	0	0	0	0	0	/	/	/	/	/
Wyoming											
Laramie County	268	0	0	0	0	0	0	0	0	0	0
Uinta County	60	0	0	0	0	0	0	0	0	0	0

/Not reported.

*No response.

[a]Allegations of abusive sexual contacts could not be counted separately from allegations of nonconsensual sexual acts.

[b]Allegations limited to substantiated occurrences only.

[c]Allegations limited to completed acts only.

[d]Based on jail population on December 31, 2006.

[e]Reports of abusive sexual contacts are not recorded in a central database.

[f]Jurisdiction does not record allegations of nonconsensual sexual acts.

[g]Jurisdiction cannot access allegations of nonconsensual sexual acts or abusive sexual contacts electronically.

Appendix table 2b. Allegations of staff-on-inmate sexual violence reported by local jail authorities, by type, 2006

Jurisdiction and facility	Reported allegations of staff sexual misconduct with inmates					Reported allegations of staff sexual harassment of inmates				
	Allega-tions	Substan-tiated	Unsubstan-tiated	Unfounded	Investiga-tion ongoing	Allega-tions	Substan-tiated	Unsub-stantiated	Unfounded	Investiga-tion ongoing
Total	217	58	58	66	35	35	9	11	10	5
Alabama										
Butler County[a]	0	0	0	0	0	/	/	/	/	/
Calhoun County[a]	1	1	0	0	0	/	/	/	/	/
Cullman County	0	0	0	0	0	0	0	0	0	0
Etowah County	0	0	0	0	0	1	0	0	1	0
Jefferson County[a]	1	1	0	0	0	/	/	/	/	/
She by County	0	0	0	0	0	0	0	0	0	0
Talledega County[a]	0	0	0	0	0	/	/	/	/	/
Tarrant City	0	0	0	0	0	0	0	0	0	0
Alaska										
Seward County	0	0	0	0	0	0	0	0	0	0
Kodiak City	0	0	0	0	0	0	0	0	0	0
Arizona										
Coconino County	0	0	0	0	0	0	0	0	0	0
Maricopa County[a]	3	0	1	2	0	/	/	/	/	/
Navajo County[a]	0	0	0	0	0	/	/	/	/	/
Pima County	0	0	0	0	0	0	0	0	0	0
Arkansas										
Arkansas County[a]	2	2	0	0	0	/	/	/	/	/
Johnson County[a]	0	0	0	0	0	/	/	/	/	/
Sebastian County	0	0	0	0	0	0	0	0	0	0
Siloam Springs City[b]	0	0	0	0	0	0	0	0	0	0
Washington County[a,b]	0	0	0	0	0	/	/	/	/	/
California										
Alameda County	2	0	2	0	0	0	0	0	0	0
Contra Costa County	1	1	0	0	0	0	0	0	0	0
El Dorado County	0	0	0	0	0	0	0	0	0	0
Fresno County[a]	1	0	0	1	0	/	/	/	/	/
Kern County	2	0	0	1	1	1	0	0	0	1
Los Angeles County	1	0	1	0	0	1	0	1	0	0
Orange County	0	0	0	0	0	0	0	0	0	0
Riverside County	0	0	0	0	0	0	0	0	0	0
Sacramento County	0	0	0	0	0	0	0	0	0	0
San Bernardino County West Valley[a]	0	0	0	0	0	/	/	/	/	/
San Diego County	0	0	0	0	0	0	0	0	0	0
San Francisco City	0	0	0	0	0	0	0	0	0	0
San Joaquin County[a]	0	0	0	0	0	/	/	/	/	/
San Luis Obispo County[a]	0	0	0	0	0	/	/	/	/	/
San Mateo County	0	0	0	0	0	0	0	0	0	0
Santa Barbara County	1	1	0	0	0	1	1	0	0	0
Santa Clara County[a]	1	0	0	0	1	/	/	/	/	/
Santa Clara County Mountain View	0	0	0	0	0	0	0	0	0	0
Santa Cruz County[a]	0	0	0	0	0	/	/	/	/	/
Ventura County	0	0	0	0	0	0	0	0	0	0
Yuba County	0	0	0	0	0	0	0	0	0	0
Colorado										
Arapahoe County	5	0	0	5	0	0	0	0	0	0
Boulder County	0	0	0	0	0	0	0	0	0	0
Denver County[b]	0	0	0	0	0	3	0	0	2	1
El Paso County	0	0	0	0	0	0	0	0	0	0
Logan County	0	0	0	0	0	0	0	0	0	0
Pueblo County	0	0	0	0	0	0	0	0	0	0
Rio Grande County[a,b]	0	0	0	0	0	/	/	/	/	/
District of Columbia										
District of Columbia	10	0	2	0	8	0	0	0	0	0

Appendix table 2b. Allegations of staff-on-inmate sexual violence reported by local jail authorities, by type, 2006

Jurisdiction and facility	Reported allegations of staff sexual misconduct with inmates					Reported allegations of staff sexual harassment of inmates				
	Allega-tions	Substan-tiated	Unsub-stantiated	Unfounded	Investiga-tion ongoing	Allega-tions	Substan-tiated	Unsub-stantiated	Unfounded	Investiga-tion ongoing
Florida										
Alachua County	0	0	0	0	0	0	0	0	0	0
Broward County	5	1	2	1	1	1	0	0	1	0
Escambia County	1	0	0	1	0	0	0	0	0	0
Highlands County	0	0	0	0	0	0	0	0	0	0
Hillsborough County	0	0	0	0	0	0	0	0	0	0
Indian River County[a]	0	0	0	0	0	/	/	/	/	/
Jackson County	0	0	0	0	0	0	0	0	0	0
Jacksonville City	0	0	0	0	0	0	0	0	0	0
Lee County	0	0	0	0	0	0	0	0	0	0
Manatee County	1	0	0	1	0	0	0	0	0	0
Marion County	0	0	0	0	0	0	0	0	0	0
Martin County	0	0	0	0	0	0	0	0	0	0
Miami-Dade County[a]	12	2	1	5	4	/	/	/	/	/
Orange County	0	0	0	0	0	0	0	0	0	0
Palm Beach County[a]	0	0	0	0	0	/	/	/	/	/
Pinellas County	0	0	0	0	0	0	0	0	0	0
Polk County	1	0	0	1	0	0	0	0	0	0
St Lucie County	2	2	0	0	0	0	0	0	0	0
Seminole County	0	0	0	0	0	0	0	0	0	0
Taylor County	0	0	0	0	0	0	0	0	0	0
Volusia County	2	1	1	0	0	0	0	0	0	0
Georgia										
Atlanta City	0	0	0	0	0	0	0	0	0	0
Bibb County	0	0	0	0	0	1	0	1	0	0
Carroll County Corr. Inst.[a]	0	0	0	0	0	/	/	/	/	/
Carroll County	0	0	0	0	0	0	0	0	0	0
Chatham County	0	0	0	0	0	1	0	0	0	1
Clayton County[a]	0	0	0	0	0	/	/	/	/	/
Clinch County	0	0	0	0	0	0	0	0	0	0
Cobb County	0	0	0	0	0	0	0	0	0	0
DeKalb County[a]	1	0	0	1	0	/	/	/	/	/
Dougherty County	0	0	0	0	0	0	0	0	0	0
Fulton County	2	1	1	0	0	0	0	0	0	0
Glynn County	0	0	0	0	0	0	0	0	0	0
Gwinnett County	0	0	0	0	0	0	0	0	0	0
Houston County	0	0	0	0	0	0	0	0	0	0
Jackson County	0	0	0	0	0	0	0	0	0	0
Lamar County[a]	0	0	0	0	0	/	/	/	/	/
Lee County	1	1	0	0	0	0	0	0	0	0
Murray County	0	0	0	0	0	0	0	0	0	0
Muscogee County[a,b]	0	0	0	0	0	/	/	/	/	/
Newton County	0	0	0	0	0	0	0	0	0	0
Rockdale County	*	*	*	*	*	*	*	*	*	*
Spalding County	0	0	0	0	0	0	0	0	0	0
Idaho										
Benewah County	0	0	0	0	0	0	0	0	0	0
Canyon County	2	2	0	0	0	0	0	0	0	0
Kootenai County	0	0	0	0	0	0	0	0	0	0
Illinois										
Champaign County	0	0	0	0	0	0	0	0	0	0
Cook County[a]	1	0	1	0	0	/	/	/	/	/
Du Page County	0	0	0	0	0	0	0	0	0	0
Lake County	0	0	0	0	0	0	0	0	0	0
McLean County	0	0	0	0	0	0	0	0	0	0
St Clair County[a,b]	0	0	0	0	0	/	/	/	/	/
Schuyler County	0	0	0	0	0	0	0	0	0	0
Whiteside County[a]	0	0	0	0	0	/	/	/	/	/

Appendix table 2b. Allegations of staff-on-inmate sexual violence reported by local jail authorities, by type, 2006

Jurisdiction and facility	Reported allegations of staff sexual misconduct with inmates					Reported allegations of staff sexual harassment of inmates				
	Allega-tions	Substan-tiated	Unsubstan-tiated	Unfounded	Investiga-tion ongoing	Allega-tions	Substan-tiated	Unsubstan-tiated	Unfounded	Investiga-tion ongoing
Indiana										
Allen County	2	2	0	0	0	0	0	0	0	0
Howard County	0	0	0	0	0	0	0	0	0	0
Kosciusko County[a]	0	0	0	0	0	/	/	/	/	/
Lake County[a]	0	0	0	0	0	/	/	/	/	/
La Porte County	0	0	0	0	0	0	0	0	0	0
Marion County[a]	0	0	0	0	0	/	/	/	/	/
Montgomery County	0	0	0	0	0	0	0	0	0	0
Porter County	0	0	0	0	0	0	0	0	0	0
Pulaski County	1	1	0	0	0	0	0	0	0	0
Union County	0	0	0	0	0	1	0	1	0	0
Iowa										
Adams County	0	0	0	0	0	0	0	0	0	0
Dubuque County[a]	0	0	0	0	0	/	/	/	/	/
Jasper County	0	0	0	0	0	0	0	0	0	0
Linn County[c]	0	0	0	0	0	/	/	/	/	/
Kansas										
Crawford County	0	0	0	0	0	0	0	0	0	0
Graham County[c,d]	/	/	/	/	/	/	/	/	/	/
Johnson County	0	0	0	0	0	0	0	0	0	0
Meade County	0	0	0	0	0	0	0	0	0	0
Shawnee County	6	3	0	3	0	1	1	0	0	0
Kentucky										
Calloway County[b]	0	0	0	0	0	0	0	0	0	0
Estill County	0	0	0	0	0	0	0	0	0	0
Franklin County	0	0	0	0	0	0	0	0	0	0
Kenton County	1	1	0	0	0	0	0	0	0	0
Laurel County[a]	0	0	0	0	0	/	/	/	/	/
Lexington-Fayette County	1	0	1	0	0	0	0	0	0	0
Louisville Metropolitan Dept. of Corr.	1	0	0	1	0	1	0	1	0	0
Pulaski County[c,d]	/	/	/	/	/	/	/	/	/	/
Rockcastle County	0	0	0	0	0	0	0	0	0	0
Warren County	0	0	0	0	0	0	0	0	0	0
Louisiana										
Bayou Dorcheat Corr. Ctr.	0	0	0	0	0	0	0	0	0	0
East Baton Rouge Prison	0	0	0	0	0	0	0	0	0	0
Grant Parish	0	0	0	0	0	0	0	0	0	0
Jefferson Parish	0	0	0	0	0	0	0	0	0	0
Madison Corr. Ctr.[b]	0	0	0	0	0	0	0	0	0	0
Ouachita Parish	0	0	0	0	0	0	0	0	0	0
New Orleans Parish[a]	1	0	1	0	0	/	/	/	/	/
St. Charles Parish	0	0	0	0	0	0	0	0	0	0
St. Tammany Parish[b]	0	0	0	0	0	0	0	0	0	0
Tangipahoa Parish	0	0	0	0	0	0	0	0	0	0
Union Parish	0	0	0	0	0	0	0	0	0	0
Vermilion Parish	0	0	0	0	0	0	0	0	0	0
Terrebonne Parish	0	0	0	0	0	0	0	0	0	0
Maine										
Cumberland County	1	0	1	0	0	0	0	0	0	0
York County	0	0	0	0	0	0	0	0	0	0
Maryland										
Allegany County	0	0	0	0	0	0	0	0	0	0
Baltimore City	3	0	1	1	1	0	0	0	0	0
Baltimore County	0	0	0	0	0	0	0	0	0	0
Frederick County[a]	2	0	1	1	0	/	/	/	/	/
Prince Georges County	0	0	0	0	0	0	0	0	0	0
Washington County	0	0	0	0	0	0	0	0	0	0
Worcester County[a]	0	0	0	0	0	/	/	/	/	/

Appendix table 2b. Allegations of staff-on-inmate sexual violence reported by local jail authorities, by type, 2006

Jurisdiction and facility	Reported allegations of staff sexual misconduct with inmates					Reported allegations of staff sexual harassment of inmates				
	Allega-tions	Substanti-ated	Unsub-stantiated	Unfounded	Investiga-tion ongoing	Allega-tions	Substanti-ated	Unsub-stantiated	Unfounded	Investiga-tion ongoing
Massachusetts										
Berkshire County	1	1	0	0	0	0	0	0	0	0
Essex County[a]	0	0	0	0	0	/	/	/	/	/
Hampden County	6	5	0	1	0	1	0	1	0	0
Plymouth County	0	0	0	0	0	0	0	0	0	0
Suffo k County	1	0	0	1	0	1	0	0	0	1
Worcester County	0	0	0	0	0	0	0	0	0	0
Michigan										
Allegan County	0	0	0	0	0	0	0	0	0	0
Genesee County	1	0	0	1	0	1	0	0	1	0
Gogebic County	0	0	0	0	0	0	0	0	0	0
Jackson County	0	0	0	0	0	0	0	0	0	0
Macomb County	0	0	0	0	0	0	0	0	0	0
Monroe County	0	0	0	0	0	0	0	0	0	0
Oakland County[a]	1	0	1	0	0	/	/	/	/	/
Ottawa County	0	0	0	0	0	0	0	0	0	0
Wayne County	0	0	0	0	0	0	0	0	0	0
Minnesota										
Hennepin County	0	0	0	0	0	0	0	0	0	0
Mille Lacs County	0	0	0	0	0	0	0	0	0	0
Pipestone County	0	0	0	0	0	0	0	0	0	0
Sherburne County[b]	0	0	0	0	0	0	0	0	0	0
Washington County	0	0	0	0	0	0	0	0	0	0
Mississippi										
Adams County	0	0	0	0	0	0	0	0	0	0
Desoto County	0	0	0	0	0	0	0	0	0	0
Harrison County[a]	1	0	0	1	0	/	/	/	/	/
Hinds County[a]	0	0	0	0	0	/	/	/	/	/
Humphreys County	0	0	0	0	0	0	0	0	0	0
Issaquena County	0	0	0	0	0	0	0	0	0	0
Kemper-Neshoda County Reg. Corr. Fac.	0	0	0	0	0	0	0	0	0	0
Leake County	0	0	0	0	0	0	0	0	0	0
Winston/Chocktaw Reg. Corr. Fac.	0	0	0	0	0	0	0	0	0	0
Missouri										
Cass County	1	0	1	0	0	0	0	0	0	0
Howard County	0	0	0	0	0	0	0	0	0	0
Lincoln County	0	0	0	0	0	0	0	0	0	0
St Charles County	0	0	0	0	0	1	1	0	0	0
St. Louis City	0	0	0	0	0	0	0	0	0	0
St. Louis County	1	1	0	0	0	0	0	0	0	0
Taney County	0	0	0	0	0	0	0	0	0	0
Vernon County	0	0	0	0	0	0	0	0	0	0
Montana										
Anaconda-Deer Lodge County[a]	0	0	0	0	0	/	/	/	/	/
Cascade County	2	1	1	0	0	0	0	0	0	0
Yellowstone County[a]	0	0	0	0	0	/	/	/	/	/
Nebraska										
Clay County	0	0	0	0	0	0	0	0	0	0
Douglas County	1	0	1	0	0	1	0	0	1	0
Lancaster County	0	0	0	0	0	0	0	0	0	0
Nevada										
Clark County	0	0	0	0	0	0	0	0	0	0
Las Vegas City[a,d]	/	/	/	/	/	/	/	/	/	/
Washoe County	1	0	0	1	0	0	0	0	0	0
New Hampshire										
Rockingham County	0	0	0	0	0	0	0	0	0	0

Appendix table 2b. Allegations of staff-on-inmate sexual violence reported by local jail authorities, by type, 2006

Jurisdiction and facility	Reported allegations of staff sexual misconduct with inmates					Reported allegations of staff sexual harassment of inmates				
	Allega-tions	Substan-tiated	Unsub-stantiated	Unfounded	Investiga-tion ongoing	Allega-tions	Substan-tiated	Unsub-stantiated	Unfounded	Investiga-tion ongoing
New Jersey										
Atlantic County[a]	0	0	0	0	0	/	/	/	/	/
Camden County	0	0	0	0	0	0	0	0	0	0
Cape May County[a]	0	0	0	0	0	/	/	/	/	/
Cumberland County	0	0	0	0	0	0	0	0	0	0
Essex County	0	0	0	0	0	0	0	0	0	0
Gloucester County	0	0	0	0	0	0	0	0	0	0
Hudson County[a]	1	0	1	0	0	/	/	/	/	/
Passaic County	0	0	0	0	0	0	0	0	0	0
Union County	0	0	0	0	0	0	0	0	0	0
New Mexico										
Bernalillo County[a]	5	3	1	1	0	/	/	/	/	/
Dona Ana County	1	0	1	0	0	0	0	0	0	0
Luna County[a]	0	0	0	0	0	/	/	/	/	/
Otero County	0	0	0	0	0	0	0	0	0	0
Quay County[a]	0	0	0	0	0	/	/	/	/	/
New York										
Albany County	0	0	0	0	0	0	0	0	0	0
Allegany County[b]	0	0	0	0	0	0	0	0	0	0
Broome County	0	0	0	0	0	0	0	0	0	0
Dutchess County	0	0	0	0	0	0	0	0	0	0
Erie County	0	0	0	0	0	0	0	0	0	0
Montgomery County	0	0	0	0	0	0	0	0	0	0
Nassau County	1	0	1	0	0	3	0	3	0	0
New York City[a]	20	0	7	10	3	/	/	/	/	/
Suffolk County	1	0	0	0	1	0	0	0	0	0
North Carolina										
Buncombe County	0	0	0	0	0	0	0	0	0	0
Cabarrus County	0	0	0	0	0	0	0	0	0	0
Carteret County[a]	0	0	0	0	0	/	/	/	/	/
Cumberland County[a]	0	0	0	0	0	/	/	/	/	/
Gaston County[a]	0	0	0	0	0	/	/	/	/	/
Mecklenburg County	2	0	1	1	0	0	0	0	0	0
Rockingham County	0	0	0	0	0	0	0	0	0	0
Swain County	1	0	0	0	1	0	0	0	0	0
Wake County	0	0	0	0	0	0	0	0	0	0
North Dakota										
Burleigh County	0	0	0	0	0	0	0	0	0	0
Rolette County	0	0	0	0	0	0	0	0	0	0
Ohio										
Cuyahoga County	4	1	2	1	0	0	0	0	0	0
Franklin County	1	0	1	0	0	0	0	0	0	0
Greene County	1	1	0	0	0	0	0	0	0	0
Hamilton County	0	0	0	0	0	0	0	0	0	0
Logan County	0	0	0	0	0	0	0	0	0	0
Lorain County	0	0	0	0	0	0	0	0	0	0
Montgomery County[a]	0	0	0	0	0	/	/	/	/	/
Noble County	0	0	0	0	0	0	0	0	0	0
Northwest Ohio Reg. Corr. Ctr.[a]	1	0	0	1	0	/	/	/	/	/
Richland County	0	0	0	0	0	0	0	0	0	0
Warren County	1	1	0	0	0	0	0	0	0	0
Oklahoma										
Garfield County	1	0	0	0	1	0	0	0	0	0
Grady County	0	0	0	0	0	0	0	0	0	0
Harmon County[c,d]	/	/	/	/	/	/	/	/	/	/
Oklahoma County	0	0	0	0	0	0	0	0	0	0
Pawnee County	0	0	0	0	0	0	0	0	0	0
Oregon										
Marion County	0	0	0	0	0	0	0	0	0	0
Multnomah County	3	0	3	0	0	0	0	0	0	0
Northern Oregon Reg. Fac.[b]	0	0	0	0	0	1	0	0	1	0
Washington County	0	0	0	0	0	0	0	0	0	0

Appendix table 2b. Allegations of staff-on-inmate sexual violence reported by local jail authorities, by type, 2006

Jurisdiction and facility	Reported allegations of staff sexual misconduct with inmates					Reported allegations of staff sexual harassment of inmates				
	Allega- tions	Substan- tiated	Unsub- stantiated	Unfounded	Investiga- tion ongoing	Allega- tions	Substan- tiated	Unsub- stantiated	Unfounded	Investiga- tion ongoing
Pennsylvania										
Allegheny County	2	0	2	0	0	0	0	0	0	0
Beaver County	*	*	*	*	*	*	*	*	*	*
Berks County	0	0	0	0	0	0	0	0	0	0
Bucks County	0	0	0	0	0	0	0	0	0	0
Clinton County	0	0	0	0	0	0	0	0	0	0
Erie County	0	0	0	0	0	0	0	0	0	0
Lycoming County	*	*	*	*	*	*	*	*	*	*
Philadelphia Prison System[a]	16	8	0	0	8	/	/	/	/	/
Schuykill County	0	0	0	0	0	0	0	0	0	0
Warren County	0	0	0	0	0	0	0	0	0	0
Westmoreland County	0	0	0	0	0	0	0	0	0	0
York County[a,b]	0	0	0	0	0	/	/	/	/	/
South Carolina										
Anderson County[a]	0	0	0	0	0	/	/	/	/	/
Charleston County	7	0	2	4	1	0	0	0	0	0
Cherokee County	0	0	0	0	0	0	0	0	0	0
Greenville County	*	*	*	*	*	*	*	*	*	*
Mar boro County	0	0	0	0	0	0	0	0	0	0
Spartanburg County	0	0	0	0	0	1	0	0	1	0
Sumter-Lee Reg. Det. Ctr.	0	0	0	0	0	0	0	0	0	0
South Dakota										
Charles Mix County	0	0	0	0	0	0	0	0	0	0
Pennington County	0	0	0	0	0	1	0	0	1	0
Tennessee										
Blount County[a]	0	0	0	0	0	/	/	/	/	/
Cheatham County[a]	0	0	0	0	0	/	/	/	/	/
Clay County	0	0	0	0	0	0	0	0	0	0
Davidson County	7	1	4	2	0	3	2	1	0	0
Madison County	0	0	0	0	0	0	0	0	0	0
Marion County[a]	0	0	0	0	0	/	/	/	/	/
McMinn County[b]	0	0	0	0	0	0	0	0	0	0
Shelby County Corr. Ctr.	1	1	0	0	0	0	0	0	0	0
Shelby County Justice Ctr.	0	0	0	0	0	0	0	0	0	0
Sullivan County	0	0	0	0	0	0	0	0	0	0
Washington County	0	0	0	0	0	0	0	0	0	0
Texas										
Bell County	0	0	0	0	0	0	0	0	0	0
Bexar County[a]	1	1	0	0	0	/	/	/	/	/
Culberson County	0	0	0	0	0	0	0	0	0	0
Dallas County	0	0	0	0	0	0	0	0	0	0
Denton County	0	0	0	0	0	0	0	0	0	0
Ector County	0	0	0	0	0	0	0	0	0	0
Ellis County	*	*	*	*	*	*	*	*	*	*
El Paso County[a]	1	0	0	0	1	/	/	/	/	/
Harris County	0	0	0	0	0	1	1	0	0	0
Hays County[a]	0	0	0	0	0	/	/	/	/	/
Hidalgo County	0	0	0	0	0	0	0	0	0	0
Live Oak County	0	0	0	0	0	0	0	0	0	0
McLennan County	0	0	0	0	0	0	0	0	0	0
Milam County[a]	0	0	0	0	0	/	/	/	/	/
Montgomery County	1	0	0	0	1	0	0	0	0	0
Orange County[a]	0	0	0	0	0	/	/	/	/	/
Rusk County[a]	0	0	0	0	0	/	/	/	/	/
Tarrant County[c]	1	1	0	0	0	/	/	/	/	/
Tom Green County[a]	0	0	0	0	0	/	/	/	/	/
Travis County	2	1	0	1	0	2	2	0	0	0
Wa ker County[a]	0	0	0	0	0	/	/	/	/	/
Webb County[a]	0	0	0	0	0	/	/	/	/	/
Wharton County[a]	0	0	0	0	0	/	/	/	/	/
Wichita County[a]	0	0	0	0	0	/	/	/	/	/

Appendix table 2b. Allegations of staff-on-inmate sexual violence reported by local jail authorities, by type, 2006									
	Reported allegations of staff sexual misconduct with inmates					Reported allegations of staff sexual harassment of inmates				
Jurisdiction and facility	Allega-tions	Substan-tiated	Unsub-stantiated	Unfounded	Investiga-tion ongoing	Allega-tions	Substan-tiated	Unsubstan-tiated	Unfounded	Investiga-tion ongoing
Utah										
Daggett County	0	0	0	0	0	0	0	0	0	0
Davis County	0	0	0	0	0	0	0	0	0	0
Salt Lake County	4	2	0	2	0	0	0	0	0	0
Weber County	0	0	0	0	0	0	0	0	0	0
Virginia										
Abingdon Reg. Jail Fac.	0	0	0	0	0	0	0	0	0	0
Augusta County	0	0	0	0	0	0	0	0	0	0
Blue Ridge Reg. Jail Auth.	1	0	1	0	0	1	0	1	0	0
Gloucester County	0	0	0	0	0	0	0	0	0	0
Middle River Reg. Jail	0	0	0	0	0	0	0	0	0	0
New River Valley Reg. Jail	1	0	0	1	0	1	0	0	1	0
Norfolk City	0	0	0	0	0	0	0	0	0	0
Northern Neck Reg. Jail	0	0	0	0	0	0	0	0	0	0
Peumansend Creek Reg. Jail[a,b]	0	0	0	0	0	/	/	/	/	/
Portsmouth City[b]	0	0	0	0	0	0	0	0	0	0
Prince William-Manassas Reg. Adult Corr. Ctr.[b]	1	0	0	1	0	0	0	0	0	0
Richmond City	0	0	0	0	0	0	0	0	0	0
Riverside Reg. Jail	6	0	2	4	0	0	0	0	0	0
Virginia Beach Municipal[a]	0	0	0	0	0	/	/	/	/	/
Washington										
Clark County	1	0	0	1	0	0	0	0	0	0
Cowlitz County	1	0	0	1	0	0	0	0	0	0
Issaquah County	0	0	0	0	0	0	0	0	0	0
King County	11	2	4	3	2	1	0	0	0	1
Pierce County[c]	0	0	0	0	0	/	/	/	/	/
Spokane County	1	1	0	0	0	0	0	0	0	0
Whatcom County	1	0	0	1	0	0	0	0	0	0
West Virgina										
Eastern Reg. Jail	0	0	0	0	0	0	0	0	0	0
Marshall County Northern Reg. Jail & Corr. Complex	0	0	0	0	0	0	0	0	0	0
North Central Reg. Jail	0	0	0	0	0	1	0	1	0	0
Raleigh County Southern Reg. Jail	5	2	3	0	0	1	1	0	0	0
Wisconsin										
Dane County	0	0	0	0	0	0	0	0	0	0
Jefferson County	0	0	0	0	0	0	0	0	0	0
Milwaukee County	0	0	0	0	0	0	0	0	0	0
Milwaukee County House of Corr.[a]	0	0	0	0	0	/	/	/	/	/
Outagamie County	0	0	0	0	0	0	0	0	0	0
Racine County	0	0	0	0	0	0	0	0	0	0
Vernon County	0	0	0	0	0	0	0	0	0	0
Walworth County[a]	1	0	1	0	0	/	/	/	/	/
Wyoming										
Laramie County	0	0	0	0	0	0	0	0	0	0
Uinta County	2	1	0	1	0	0	0	0	0	0

/Not reported.

*No response.

[a]Allegations of staff sexual harrassment could not be counted separately from allegations of staff sexual misconduct.

[b]Reports of staff sexual misconduct are based on substantiated allegations only.

[c]Reports of staff sexual harrassment are not recorded in a central database.

[d]Reports of staff sexual misconduct are not recorded in a central database.

Appendix table 3a. Allegations of inmate-on-inmate sexual violence reported in private prisons and jails, 2006

Jurisdiction and facility	Average daily population, 2006	Reported inmate-on-inmate nonconsensual sexual acts					Reported inmate-on-inmate abusive sexual contacts				
		Allegations	Substantiated	Unsubstantiated	Unfounded	Investigation ongoing	Allegations	Substantiated	Unsubstantiated	Unfounded	Investigation ongoing
Total	48,594	51	1	19	28	3	6	0	5	0	1
Arizona											
Eloy Det. Ctr. (CCA)[a]	1,241	0	0	0	0	0	/	/	/	/	/
Phoenix CCC (BSS)[a]	94	0	0	0	0	0	/	/	/	/	/
California											
California City Corr. Ctr. (CCA)	2,603	0	0	0	0	0	0	0	0	0	0
Central Valley Community Corr. (GEO)	600	0	0	0	0	0	0	0	0	0	0
San Diego County Probation Dept. (CAI)	148	0	0	0	0	0	0	0	0	0	0
Taft Corr. Inst. (GEO)	2,330	0	0	0	0	0	0	0	0	0	0
Colorado											
Cheyenne Martain Re-Entry Ctr. (CEC)	467	0	0	0	0	0	0	0	0	0	0
Crowley County Corr. Fac. (CCA)	1,277	1	0	1	0	0	0	0	0	0	0
Longmont Community Treatment Ctr. (CMI)	62	0	0	0	0	0	0	0	0	0	0
Florida											
Bay Corr. Inst. (CCA)	747	0	0	0	0	0	0	0	0	0	0
Bay County Jail & Annex (CCA)	850	0	0	0	0	0	1	0	1	0	0
South Bay Corr. Fac. (GEO)	1,856	2	0	2	0	0	0	0	0	0	0
Suncoast Work Release Ctr. (Goodwill)	105	0	0	0	0	0	0	0	0	0	0
Georgia											
Coffee Corr. Fac. (CCA)	1,680	13	0	0	13	0	2	0	2	0	0
D. Ray James Prison (Cornell)	1,640	1	0	0	0	1	1	0	0	0	1
McRae Corr. Fac. (CCA)	1,665	0	0	0	0	0	0	0	0	0	0
Kentucky											
Owensboro (Dismas)	132	0	0	0	0	0	0	0	0	0	0
Louisiana											
Allen Corr. Ctr. (GEO)[a,b]	1,540	0	0	0	0	0	/	/	/	/	/
Minnesota											
Prairie Corr. Fac. (CCA)	1,480	0	0	0	0	0	0	0	0	0	0
Mississippi											
East Mississippi Corr. Fac. (GEO)[c]	857	0	0	0	0	0	/	/	/	/	/
Tallahatchie County Corr. Fac. (CCA)	1,002	1	0	0	1	0	0	0	0	0	0
Wi kinson County Corr. Fac. (CCA)	946	4	0	2	2	0	0	0	0	0	0
Montana											
Crossroads Corr. Ctr. (CCA)[a]	504	1	0	0	1	0	/	/	/	/	/
Nevada											
Cornell Corr. (Cornell)[a]	75	0	0	0	0	0	/	/	/	/	/
New Jersey											
Kintock I, II, III (Kintock)[a]	595	0	0	0	0	0	/	/	/	/	/
New Mexico											
New Mexico Women's Corr. Fac. (CCA)[b]	616	0	0	0	0	0	0	0	0	0	0

Appendix table 3a. Allegations of inmate-on-inmate sexual violence reported in private prisons and jails, 2006 (cont.)

Jurisdiction and facility	Average daily population, 2006	Reported inmate-on-inmate nonconsensual sexual acts					Reported inmate-on-inmate abusive sexual contacts				
		Allegations	Substantiated	Unsubstantiated	Unfounded	Investigation ongoing	Allegations	Substantiated	Unsubstantiated	Unfounded	Investigation ongoing
Ohio											
Fresh Start, Inc.	85	0	0	0	0	0	0	0	0	0	0
Lake Erie Corr. Inst. (MTC)	1,464	0	0	0	0	0	0	0	0	0	0
Oklahoma											
Center Point, Inc.[a]	150	0	0	0	0	0	/	/	/	/	/
Cimarron Corr. Fac. (CCA)	963	3	1	1	1	0	0	0	0	0	0
Diamondback Corr. Fac. (CCA)	1,980	1	0	1	0	0	0	0	0	0	0
Lawton Corr. Fac. (GEO)[a]	2,016	10	0	5	3	2	/	/	/	/	/
Pennsylvania											
George W. Hill Corr. Fac. (GEO)	1,801	0	0	0	0	0	0	0	0	0	0
Kintock Pre-Release (Kintock)	283	0	0	0	0	0	0	0	0	0	0
Tennessee											
Hardeman County Corr. Ctr. (CCA)[b]	1,966	0	0	0	0	0	0	0	0	0	0
Metro Davidson County Det. Fac. (CCA)	992	0	0	0	0	0	0	0	0	0	0
South Central Corr. Ctr. (CCA)	1,634	3	0	0	3	0	0	0	0	0	0
Texas											
Bartlett (CCA)	996	0	0	0	0	0	0	0	0	0	0
B.M. Moore (CCA)	498	0	0	0	0	0	0	0	0	0	0
Bridgeport Pre-Parole Fac. (CCA)	519	0	0	0	0	0	0	0	0	0	0
Dawson State Jail (CCA)[a]	2,182	0	0	0	0	0	/	/	/	/	/
Dickens County Corr. Ctr. (GEO)[a]	474	0	0	0	0	0	/	/	/	/	/
Mineral Wells Pre-Parole Fac. (CCA)[a]	2,075	1	0	0	1	0	/	/	/	/	/
Reeves County Det. Ctr. (GEO)	780	6	0	6	0	0	2	0	2	0	0
Willacy County State Jail (CCA)[a]	1,057	3	0	0	3	0	/	/	/	/	/
Virginia											
Lawrenceville Corr. Ctr. (GEO)	1,567	1	0	1	0	0	0	0	0	0	0

Note: Initials identify the following: BSS - Behavioral Systems Southwest. CAI - Correctional Alternatives Incorporated. CCA - Corrections Corporation of America. CEC - Community Education Center. CMI - Correctional Management, Inc. Cornell - Cornell Companies, Incorporated. GEO - Global Expertise in Outsourcing. MTC - Management and Training Corporation.

/Not reported.

[a]Allegations of abusive sexual contacts could not be counted separately from allegations of nonconsensual sexual acts.

[b]Allegations limited to substantiated occurrences only.

[c]Does not record allegations of abusive sexual contact in a central database.

Appendix table 3b. Allegations of staff-on-inmate sexual violence reported in private prisons and jails, by type, 2006

Jurisdiction and facility	Reported allegations of staff sexual misconduct with inmates					Reported allegations of staff sexual harassment of inmates				
	Allegations	Substantiated	Unsubstantiated	Unfounded	Investigation ongoing	Allegations	Substantiated	Unsubstantiated	Unfounded	Investigation ongoing
Total	39	6	21	7	5	11	0	3	0	8
Arizona										
Eloy Det. Ctr. (CCA)[a]	0	0	0	0	0	/	/	/	/	/
Phoenix CCC (BSS)[a,b]	0	0	0	0	0	/	/	/	/	/
California										
California City Corr. Ctr. (CCA)	1	0	0	1	0	0	0	0	0	0
Central Valley Community Corr. (GEO)	0	0	0	0	0	0	0	0	0	0
San Diego County Probation Dept. (CAI)	0	0	0	0	0	0	0	0	0	0
Taft Corr. Inst. (GEO)	1	0	1	0	0	0	0	0	0	0
Colorado										
Cheyenne Martain Re-Entry Ctr. (CEC)	0	0	0	0	0	0	0	0	0	0
Crowley County Corr. Fac. (CCA)	0	0	0	0	0	0	0	0	0	0
Longmont Community Treatment Ctr. (CMI)	0	0	0	0	0	0	0	0	0	0
Florida										
Bay Corr. Inst. (CCA)	1	0	0	1	0	0	0	0	0	0
Bay County Jail & Annex (CCA)	0	0	0	0	0	0	0	0	0	0
South Bay Corr. Fac. (GEO)	0	0	0	0	0	0	0	0	0	0
Suncoast Work Release Ctr. (Goodwill)	0	0	0	0	0	0	0	0	0	0
Georgia										
Coffee Corr. Fac. (CCA)	11	0	11	0	0	0	0	0	0	0
D. Ray James Prison (Cornell)	4	0	0	0	4	8	0	0	0	8
McRae Corr. Fac. (CCA)	2	1	1	0	0	0	0	0	0	0
Kentucky										
Owensboro (Dismas)	0	0	0	0	0	0	0	0	0	0
Louisiana										
Allen Corr. Ctr. (GEO)[b]	0	0	0	0	0	0	0	0	0	0
Minnesota										
Prairie Corr. Fac. (CCA)	2	0	0	1	1	0	0	0	0	0
Mississippi										
East Mississippi Corr. Fac. (GEO)	0	0	0	0	0	0	0	0	0	0
Tallahatchie County Corr. Fac. (CCA)	1	0	0	1	0	0	0	0	0	0
Wilkinson County Corr. Fac. (CCA)	0	0	0	0	0	0	0	0	0	0
Montana										
Crossroads Corr. Ctr. (CCA)[a]	0	0	0	0	0	/	/	/	/	/
Nevada										
Cornell Corr. (Cornell)[a]	0	0	0	0	0	/	/	/	/	/
New Jersey										
Kintock I, II, III (Kintock)	0	0	0	0	0	0	0	0	0	0
New Mexico										
New Mexico Women's Corr. Fac. (CCA)	0	0	0	0	0	0	0	0	0	0
Ohio										
Fresh Start, Inc.	0	0	0	0	0	0	0	0	0	0
Lake Erie Corr. Inst. (MTC)	0	0	0	0	0	0	0	0	0	0

Appendix table 3b. Allegations of staff-on-inmate sexual violence reported in private prisons and jails, by type, 2006 (cont.)

	Reported allegations of staff sexual misconduct with inmates					Reported allegations of staff sexual harassment of inmates				
Jurisdiction and facility	Allega-tions	Substan-tiated	Unsubstan-tiated	Unfounded	Investiga-tion ongoing	Allega-tions	Substan-tiated	Unsubstan-tiated	Unfounded	Investiga-tion ongoing
Oklahoma										
Center Point, Inc.	1	0	0	1	0	0	0	0	0	0
Cimarron Corr. Fac. (CCA)	1	0	1	0	0	0	0	0	0	0
Diamondback Corr. Fac. (CCA)	4	1	3	0	0	0	0	0	0	0
Lawton Corr. Fac. (GEO)[a]	3	2	0	1	0	/	/	/	/	/
Pennsylvania										
George W. Hill Corr. Fac. (GEO)	0	0	0	0	0	0	0	0	0	0
Kintock Pre-Release (Kin-tock)	0	0	0	0	0	0	0	0	0	0
Tennessee										
Hardeman County Corr. Ctr. (CCA)	0	0	0	0	0	0	0	0	0	0
Metro Davidson County Det. Fac. (CCA)	0	0	0	0	0	0	0	0	0	0
South Central Corr. Ctr. (CCA)	0	0	0	0	0	0	0	0	0	0
Texas										
Bartlett (CCA)	0	0	0	0	0	3	0	3	0	0
B.M. Moore (CCA)	1	0	1	0	0	0	0	0	0	0
Bridgeport Pre-Parole Fac. (CCA)[a]	1	0	0	1	0	/	/	/	/	/
Dawson State Jail (CCA)[a]	0	0	0	0	0	/	/	/	/	/
Dickens County Corr. Ctr. (GEO)[a]	1	1	0	0	0	/	/	/	/	/
Mineral Wells Pre-Parole Fac. (CCA)[a]	0	0	0	0	0	/	/	/	/	/
Reeves County Det. Ctr. (GEO)	1	1	0	0	0	0	0	0	0	0
Willacy County State Jail (CCA)[a]	0	0	0	0	0	/	/	/	/	/
Virginia										
Lawrenceville Corr. Ctr. (GEO)	3	0	3	0	0	0	0	0	0	0

Note: Initials identify the following: BSS - Behavioral Systems Southwest. CAI - Correctional Alternatives Incorporated. CCA - Corrections Corporation of America. CEC - Community Education Center. CMI - Correctional Management, Inc. Cornell - Cornell Companies, Incorporated. GEO - Global Expertise in Outsourcing. MTC - Management and Training Corporation.

/Not reported.

[a]Reports of staff sexual misconduct may include reports of staff sexual harassment.

[b]Reports of staff sexual misconduct are based on substantiated allegations only.

Appendix table 4a. Allegations of inmate-on-inmate sexual violence reported in other correctional facilties, by type, 2006

Jurisdiction and facility	Average daily population, 2006	Reported inmate-on-inmate nonconsensual sexual acts					Reported inmate-on-inmate abusive sexual contacts				
		Allegations	Substantiated	Unsubstantiated	Unfounded	Investigation ongoing	Allegations	Substantiated	Unsubstantiated	Unfounded	Investigation ongoing
U.S. Military											
Total	1,937	1	1	0	0	0	1	1	0	0	0
Air Force	91	0	0	0	0	0	0	0	0	0	0
Army	1,019	0	0	0	0	0	0	0	0	0	0
Marines	194	1	1	0	0	0	0	0	0	0	0
Navy	633	0	0	0	0	0	1	1	0	0	0
U.S. Immigration and Customs Enforcement											
Total	8,033	3	1	1	1	0	0	0	0	0	0
Aguadilla, PR	32	0	0	0	0	0	0	0	0	0	0
Aurora, CO	381	0	0	0	0	0	0	0	0	0	0
Batavia, NY	454	0	0	0	0	0	0	0	0	0	0
El Centro, CA	456	0	0	0	0	0	0	0	0	0	0
Elizabeth, NJ	297	0	0	0	0	0	0	0	0	0	0
El Paso, TX[a,b,c]	785	0	0	0	0	0	/	/	/	/	/
Florence, AZ[a]	617	0	0	0	0	0	/	/	/	/	/
Houston, TX[a]	830	0	0	0	0	0	/	/	/	/	/
Laredo, TX	335	0	0	0	0	0	0	0	0	0	0
Los Fresnos, TX	810	0	0	0	0	0	0	0	0	0	0
Miami, FL	677	0	0	0	0	0	0	0	0	0	0
San Diego, CA	1,196	3	1	1	1	0	0	0	0	0	0
San Pedro, CA	388	0	0	0	0	0	0	0	0	0	0
Tacoma, WA[a]	775	0	0	0	0	0	/	/	/	/	/
Jails in Indian Country											
Total	279	0	0	0	0	0	0	0	0	0	0
Gila River Dept. of Corr. & Rehab., AZ[a]	51	0	0	0	0	0	/	/	/	/	/
Hopi Rehab. Ctr., AZ	51	0	0	0	0	0	0	0	0	0	0
Klyuska O'Tipi Reintegration Ctr., SD[a]	5	0	0	0	0	0	/	/	/	/	/
Ponca Tr bal Police Dept., OK	63	0	0	0	0	0	0	0	0	0	0
Red Lake Law Enforcement Services, MN	43	0	0	0	0	0	0	0	0	0	0
Rocky Boy Police Dept., MT	7	0	0	0	0	0	0	0	0	0	0
Rosebud Sioux Tribe Law Enforcement, SD	43	0	0	0	0	0	0	0	0	0	0
Taos Tribal Det. Ctr., NM	6	0	0	0	0	0	0	0	0	0	0
Yakama Police Dept., WA	10	0	0	0	0	0	0	0	0	0	0

/Not reported.

[a]Allegations of abusive sexual contacts could not be counted separately from allegations of nonconsensual sexual acts.

[b]Allegations limited to substantiated incidents only.

[c]Allegations limited to completed acts only.

Appendix table 4b. Allegations of staff-on-inmate sexual violence reported in other correctional facilities, by type, 2006

Jurisdiction and facility	Reported allegations of staff sexual misconduct with inmates					Reported allegations of staff sexual harassment of inmates				
	Allega-tions	Substan-tiated	Unsub-stantiated	Unfounded	Investiga-tion ongoing	Allega-tions	Substan-tiated	Unsub-stantiated	Unfounded	Investigation ongoing
U.S. Military										
Total	1	0	0	0	1	0	0	0	0	0
Air Force	0	0	0	0	0	0	0	0	0	0
Army	0	0	0	0	0	0	0	0	0	0
Marines	0	0	0	0	0	0	0	0	0	0
Navy	1	0	0	0	1	0	0	0	0	0
U.S. Immigration and Customs Enforcement										
Total	1	0	1	0	0	1	1	0	0	0
Aguadilla, PR	0	0	0	0	0	0	0	0	0	0
Aurora, CO	0	0	0	0	0	0	0	0	0	0
Batavia, NY	0	0	0	0	0	0	0	0	0	0
El Centro, CA	0	0	0	0	0	0	0	0	0	0
Elizabeth, NJ	0	0	0	0	0	0	0	0	0	0
El Paso, TX	0	0	0	0	0	0	0	0	0	0
Florence, AZ	1	0	1	0	0	0	0	0	0	0
Houston, TX*	0	0	0	0	0	/	/	/	/	/
Laredo, TX	0	0	0	0	0	0	0	0	0	0
Los Fresnos, TX	0	0	0	0	0	0	0	0	0	0
Miami, FL	0	0	0	0	0	0	0	0	0	0
San Diego, CA	0	0	0	0	0	1	1	0	0	0
San Pedro, CA	0	0	0	0	0	0	0	0	0	0
Tacoma, WA	0	0	0	0	0	0	0	0	0	0
Jails in Indian Country										
Total	3	0	0	3	0	1	1	0	0	0
Gila River Dept. of Corr. & Rehab. AZ	0	0	0	0	0	0	0	0	0	0
Hopi Rehab. Ctr., AZ	0	0	0	0	0	0	0	0	0	0
Klyuska O'Tipi Reintegra-tion Ctr., SD	0	0	0	0	0	0	0	0	0	0
Ponca Tr bal Police Dept., OK	0	0	0	0	0	0	0	0	0	0
Red Lake Law Enforce-ment Services, MN	0	0	0	0	0	0	0	0	0	0
Rocky Boy Police Dept., MT	2	0	0	2	0	1	1	0	0	0
Rosebud Sioux Tribe Law Enforcement, SD	1	0	0	1	0	0	0	0	0	0
Taos Tribal Det. Ctr., NM	0	0	0	0	0	0	0	0	0	0
Yakama Police Dept., WA	0	0	0	0	0	0	0	0	0	0

/Not reported.
*Reports of staff sexual misconduct may include reports of staff sexual harassment.

Appendix table 5. Characteristics of victims in substantiated incidents of inmate-on-inmate sexual violence, by type, 2006

Characteristic	All facilities[a]	Prison	Jail
Number of incidents	410	272	132
Number of victims			
1	92%	92%	93%
2	7	8	6
3	1	<1	1
4 or more	<1	<1	0
Gender[b]			
Male	82%	80%	84%
Female	18	20	16
Age[b]			
Under 18	4%	1%	13%
18-24	40	37	44
25-29	18	21	14
30-34	12	15	6
35-39	10	7	15
40-44	6	8	3
45 or older	9	11	5
Race/Hispanic origin[b]			
White[c]	72%	76%	65%
Black[c]	16	13	21
Hispanic	9	8	12
Other[c,d]	3	3	1

[a]Includes substantiated incidents reported by private prisons and jails, Indian country jails, and facilities operated by the U.S. military and ICE.

[b]Based on characteristics of victims for whom gender (443), age (442), or race/Hispanic origin (445) were reported.

[c]Excludes perpetrators of Hispanic origin.

[d]Includes American Indians, Alaska Natives, Asians, Native Hawaiians, and Other Pacific Islanders.

Appendix table 6. Characteristics of perpetrators in substantiated incidents of inmate-on-inmate sexual violence, by type, 2006

Characteristic	All facilities[a]	Prison	Jail
Number of incidents	410	272	132
Number of perpetrators			
1	90%	90%	90%
2	6	7	5
3	2	2	5
4 or more	1	1	0
Gender[b]			
Male	85%	82%	92%
Female	15	18	8
Age[b]			
Under 18	1%	1%	0%
18-24	19	20	14
25-29	21	16	31
30-34	19	19	19
35-39	13	15	9
40-44	12	9	18
45 or older	16	19	9
Race/Hispanic origin[b]			
White[c]	39%	48%	22%
Black[c]	49	43	60
Hispanic	10	7	15
Other[c,d]	2	2	4

Note: Detail may not sum to 100% due to rounding.

[a]Includes substantiated incidents reported by private prisons and jails, Indian country jails, and facilities operated by the U.S. military and ICE.

[b]Based on characteristics of perpetrators for whom gender (448), age (443), or race/Hispanic origin (444) were reported.

[c]Excludes perpetrators of Hispanic origin.

[d]Includes American Indians, Alaska Natives, Asians, Native Hawaiians, and Other Pacific Islanders.

Appendix table 7. Circumstances surrounding substantiated incidents of inmate-on-inmate sexual violence, by type, 2006

	All facilities*	Prison	Jail	Nonconsensual sexual acts	Abusive sexual contacts
Number of incidents	409	272	131	250	159
Type of pressure or force					
None	21%	21%	18%	14%	31%
Force/threat of force	58	53	70	67	44
Threatened with physical harm	32	24	47	43	14
Physically held down or restrained	34	27	51	38	28
Physically harmed or injured	15	15	16	18	10
Threatened with a weapon	2	2	4	4	0
Persuasion or talked into it	30	32	29	32	28
Bribery/blackmail	3	3	4	3	4
Gave victim drugs/alcohol	1	<1	2	1	0
Offered protection from other inmates	3	3	3	4	1
Where occurred					
In victim's cell/room	64%	57%	79%	76%	46%
In perpetrator's cell/room	5	6	5	5	6
In a dormitory	9	10	7	6	14
In a common area	17	22	7	11	26
In temporary holding area	<1	0	1	0	1
In a program service area	6	8	2	5	6
Outside the facility	2	1	2	<1	3
While in transit	<1	<1	0	0	1
Time of day[b]					
6 a.m. to noon	20%	22%	15%	17%	24%
Noon to 6 p.m.	26	28	21	18	37
6 p.m. to midnight	45	46	41	47	41
Midnight to 6 a.m.	26	20	37	32	17
Who reported the incident					
Victim	70%	66%	75%	72%	65%
Another inmate	13	10	21	16	9
Family of victim	1	2	0	<1	2
Correctional officer	17	23	5	12	24
Administrative staff	2	1	2	0	4
Medical/healthcare staff	1	2	0	1	1
Counselor/teacher	<1	<1	0	<1	0
Chaplain/other religious official	1	1	0	1	0

Note: Detail may sum to more than 100% because multiple responses were allowed for each item.
*Includes substantiated incidents reported by private prisons and jails, Indian country jails, and facilities operated by the U.S. military and ICE.

Appendix table 8. Impact on victim and perpetrator in substantiated incidents of inmate-on-inmate sexual violence, by type, 2006

Incident impact	All facilities[a]	Prison	Jail	Nonconsensual sexual acts	Abusive sexual contacts
Victim injured					
No	80%	81%	76%	74%	87%
Yes[b]	20	19	24	26	13
Anal/vaginal tearing	5	6	5	8	1
Teeth chipped/knocked out	1	0	2	1	0
Bruises, black eye, sprains, cuts, scratches, swelling	13	12	15	14	12
Medical followup for victim					
Given medical examination	60%	54%	74%	70%	45%
Administered rape kit	22	20	28	34	3
Tested for HIV/AIDS	11	11	13	19	0
Tested for other STD	12	11	14	19	0
Provided counseling or mental health treatment	50	56	40	53	45
None of the above	22	25	16	17	30
Change in housing/custody for victim					
Placed in administrative segregation or protective custody	40%	46%	30%	45%	31%
Placed in medical unit	13	7	24	19	3
Confined to own cell/room	9	10	5	7	11
Given higher custody level	2	2	2	2	1
Transferred to another facility/elsewhere in facility	16	21	7	16	17
Other (reported after release/transfer)	6	2	15	7	4
None of the above	24	26	20	16	39
Sanction imposed on perpetrator					
Solitary/disciplinary	78%	77%	81%	81%	75%
Confined to own cell/room	16	17	13	18	12
Placed in higher custody	22	21	26	24	20
Transferred to another facility	22	25	16	24	17
Loss of good time	24	26	20	20	31
Given extra work	2	2	0	2	1
Loss of privileges	20	25	12	23	16
Legal action	41	30	67	56	18
Arrested	16	3	42	21	6
Referred for prosecution	33	26	49	46	13
Given new sentence	5	4	9	6	4
Disciplinary report issued	5	7	0	4	6

Note: Detail may sum to more than 100% because multiple responses were allowed for each item.

[a]Includes substantiated incidents reported by private prisons and jails, Indian country jails, and facilities operated by the U.S. military and ICE.

[b]The categories "knife or stab wounds," "broken bones," "internal injuries," and "knocked unconscious" were not marked in any incident.